JOURNEY
TO THE MANGER

**A REFLECTIVE DEVOTIONAL FOR
ADVENT AND CHRISTMAS**

JON JENNINGS

Scripture quotations marked (CSB) have been taken from the Christian Standard Bible®, Copyright © 2017 by Holman Bible Publishers. Used by permission. Christian Standard Bible® and CSB® are federally registered trademarks of Holman Bible Publishers.

Scripture quotations marked (NIV) are taken from the Holy Bible, New International Version®, NIV®. Copyright © 1973, 1978, 1984, 2011 by Biblica, Inc.™ Used by permission of Zondervan. All rights reserved worldwide. www.zondervan.com. The "NIV" and "New International Version" are trademarks registered in the United States Patent and Trademark Office by Biblica, Inc.™

Scripture quotations marked (NLT) are taken from the Holy Bible, New Living Translation, copyright ©1996, 2004, 2015 by Tyndale House Foundation. Used by permission of Tyndale House Publishers, a Division of Tyndale House Ministries, Carol Stream, Illinois 60188. All rights reserved.

Scripture quotations marked (ESV) are from the ESV® Bible (The Holy Bible, English Standard Version®), copyright © 2001 by Crossway, a publishing ministry of Good News Publishers. Used by permission. All rights reserved.

Scripture quotations marked (NKJV) are taken from the New King James Version®. Copyright © 1982 by Thomas Nelson. Used by permission. All rights reserved.

Scripture quotations marked (NAS) are taken from the NEW AMERICAN STANDARD BIBLE(R), Copyright (C) 1960,1962,1963,1968,1971,1972,1973,1975,1977 ,1995 by The Lockman Foundation. Used by permission.

Scripture quotations marked (MSG) are taken from THE MESSAGE. Copyright © 1993, 1994, 1995, 1996, 2000, 2001, 2002. Used by permission of NavPress Publishing Group.

First paperback edition September 2023

Cover design and formatting by Julie V. Miser
Author Photograph by Patricia Santangelo

ISBN 979-8-9888818-0-3 (paperback)
ISBN 979-8-9888818-1-0 (ebook)

jonjennings.me

For Gwen: The love of my life, best friend, and biggest cheerleader – because you stayed.

FOREWORD

WHENEVER I READ A FOREWORD to a new book, one of the first things I want to know is what does the person writing the foreword know? What do they know about the author and the subject at hand? With that in mind let me tell you a few things I know.

I have known Pastor Jon Jennings for over a decade. We met watching our boys play for their Jr. High basketball team and over the years, the Holy Spirit has connected our lives and families in a powerful way. Today we serve together as Pastors of the Pure Heart Churches in the greater Phoenix area.

Jon is a brilliant teacher and writer which is a rare combination. There are great writers who are not great teachers and great teachers who are not great writers. Jon is blessed to be both. More importantly, I have had the privilege of knowing the man. I have experienced life with Jon on the mountain top and in the darkest valley as a trusted friend and brother in his life. I was among the first to know of his greatest failure and then watched with awe as the Holy Spirit healed his soul, family, and ministry.

I also know that a large part of Jon's healing was putting into practice the spiritual discipline of silence. What you are about to experience in this devotional isn't just scholarly insight, it is born from Jon's commitment to this vital practice. As Jon shares through the lens of the Advent story, you will get the opportunity to make this story personal in your own life. I know this because Jon's commitment to daily time with Jesus has spurred me on to greater depths of quiet reflection.

I know that as a student of God's Word, Jon's passion to write this book has been burning for many years. The day he told me what the Lord had put on his heart to write, I could feel the excitement in his voice, and I know that he wants us to experience that same joy.

Finally, I know that if you slow down through the season of Advent, you will not only grow, but also be reminded how truly loved you are by God. Last Christmas, Jon gave me a devotional he was reading for Advent, and I must confess, after 25 years in ministry, this was the first time I had slowed down to personally reflect on the incarnation of Jesus. For many Pastors, Christmas is one of the busiest times of the year. For me personally, the month of December sees me preaching nearly 30 times with our online and in-person services! When adding the invites to Christmas parties and family traditions, who has time to slow down? But I did! I spent time each day reflecting on the greatest event in human history when God came near. I enjoyed Christmas 2022 more than any other year, because I slowed down, practiced silence, and drew near to Jesus. As a result, He deeply reminded me of His love.

Now, 2023 is here and I can't wait to slow down again and personally connect with the story of God's plan to redeem and restore our broken world. This devotional is filled with hope, vulnerability, practical insight, personal reflection, all anchored in the biblical journey of Advent. Enough about what I know. It's time for you to enjoy the presence of Jesus as you journey to the manger and allow God's love to refresh your soul.

Dan Steffen

Sr. Pastor - Pure Heart Churches

AUTHOR'S PREFACE AND HOW TO USE THIS DEVOTIONAL

IN OCTOBER 2018, I HIT ROCK BOTTOM. A 6-year dark night of the soul came to a climax and at age 50, I thought my life was over. Earlier that year, my wife and I celebrated 26 years of marriage and ministry together but because of my sin and a series of self-destructive choices, I had no idea if marriage or ministry would survive. The root of the problem was that I had neither developed nor sustained an interior life with God that was healthy and capable of supporting my exterior life. I loved Jesus with all my heart, but over time and while doing God's work as a Pastor and church leader, I lost my way. To find my way again, a radical shift needed to take place and through a sequence of what I believe to be supernatural events, I discovered beauty and life in the ancient practices of Silence, Solitude, and Sabbath. Implementing these practices was instrumental not only in my personal restoration, but also in the restoration of my marriage and, ultimately, the ministry God called me to.

Daily silence and solitude are intentional times set aside to simply be with Jesus. They help us distance from the noise and chaos of our world and draw near to God. With these practices, there is no agenda, prayer list, or time goals. There is only silence, scripture, prayer, and journaling. Prior to 2018, journaling had been a sporadic practice in my life, but it became a vital rhythm that is now oxygen to my soul.

Sabbath is equally life-giving as I set aside a 24-hour period each week and do nothing except stop all work, delight in God's wonder, rest in his divine goodness, and contemplate all that he is. The revolution I desperately needed began with these practices and 5-years later (at the time of this writing), I am living my best life. My 50's have turned out to be my best decade personally, in marriage, and in ministry.

This devotional was born out of my daily journal and follows the liturgical Advent calendar of the church. Growing up Pentecostal, I knew little of the historical calendar or the practices that Christians have observed for centuries, but once I discovered them, I realized that they are not empty rituals, but rather, full of life and spiritual depth. As you engage with the content in this devotional, I invite you to take a bold step and change how you engage with God daily. See yourself entering a sacred mystery where awe and wonder dominate your time.

This devotional is designed for deep reflection, not a quick fix for the day so you can check the box as you rush out the door each morning. I recommend the following practice to get the most out of the devotional content.

1. **Slow Down.** Put your devices in another room and find a serene, quiet place.
2. **Practice Silence.** This will be uncomfortable at first if you have never done it, but it helps clear out the noise and clutter that compete for our attention. Try a minute or two at first, then allow it to grow into more.

3. **Invite** Jesus to be with you. I use a modified version of the prayer of St. Patrick to help center my heart's affections and my mind's thoughts, but you can develop your own focused prayer, whatever is comfortable for you.

Christ above me, very God of very God
Christ below me, incarnate of the earth
Christ before me when I see
Christ behind me when I cannot see
Christ at my right hand in my strength
Christ at me left in my weakness
Christ in me, the hope of glory, formed by faith

4. **Read** the <u>entire</u> scripture passage for that day. Don't skim. As a Pastor and teacher, I believe at my core that context is everything, and we do ourselves a disservice by pulling random scriptures and trying to apply them apart from their context. There is a key verse for each day, but I have tried to structure the readings in such a way that you will gain at least some of the context present.

5. **Reflect** on the passage and devotional reading. Give yourself time to do this.

6. **Pray.** A short prayer is included at the end of each day's reading and is designed to be a starting point. Ask the Lord to speak into your heart the things he wants you to pray from the day's reading.

7. **Journal.** This is a difficult practice for some and life-giving for others. I encourage you to at least try this practice, as it will help you process what God is saying to you in this season and give you a way to look back on your journey.

Advent has been a rich tradition in Christianity dating back to the 5th century. "Advent" means "Arrival" or "Anticipation" and four weeks before Christmas, Advent commences with great anticipation of the arrival of the Messiah. We embrace the promise made by God that a Savior will come, and we live through the patriarchs and prophets of Israel who anticipated the fulfillment of the promise. As we join with the ancients in this journey waiting for the "fullness of time" to come (Gal. 4:4), we also anticipate Christ coming to us in fresh ways, breaking into our current circumstances to bring something new and glorious. We also anticipate his return, his second advent as promised to his followers before he ascended into heaven.

Specifics of the Advent celebration vary by tradition. I invite you to study out various traditions of Advent and choose one that is best for you. These devotional readings combine elements of both the Western and Orthodox traditions. The first reading begins four Sundays before Christmas and continues four full weeks until Christmas Day. The actual time between the start of Advent and December 25th will vary from year to year, so you may need to combine some days of readings along the way to get them all in. Following the liturgical tradition, readings continue through the twelve days of Christmas, also known as "Christmastide," ending with the Epiphany on January 6th.

In this Advent season, may you capture the awe, joy, and wonder of the incarnation as we journey to the manger.

Grace to you all.

Jon Jennings (Glendale, AZ 2023)

JOURNEY
TO THE MANGER
A REFLECTIVE DEVOTIONAL FOR ADVENT AND CHRISTMAS

FIRST WEEK OF ADVENT
SUNDAY
"THE FIRST GOSPEL"

Reading: Genesis 3:1-15

"I will put hostility between you and the woman, and between your offspring and her offspring. He will strike your head, and you will strike his heel."

GENESIS 3:15 (CSB)

I AM A SUCKER FOR A GREAT STORY. It doesn't matter if the story is told through a novel, movie, podcast, talk show, or in casual conversation. A great story is captivating and draws us into its world. If a story is told right, it activates our senses and makes us feel as if we are part of the plot. Research has shown our brains light up when we listen to a story and as it unfolds, our brain waves begin to synchronize with those of the storyteller. Emotional attachments are created as we identify with the story and soon, we find ourselves not only in the story but also moved to action.

God's word is that kind of story. It is His story and our story together as one. The pages of scripture unfold an epic account of paradise lost, and paradise regained, exile and return, tragedy and triumph, defeat and victory, adversity and opportunity, despair, and hope. The story begins in the perfection of Eden's Garden with God and humanity joined in an untarnished relationship but quickly descends into a lonely wilderness where the relationship is severed because of the serpent's deception and humanity's rebellion. As the story continues, we meet people just like us, deeply flawed, and striving on their own to undo the mess and restore the lost relationship with their Creator. All self-driven efforts, however, prove to be futile and hopeless. Through unparalleled adventure, the story ends as it began, but this time in a perfect city where humanity once again enjoys an untarnished relationship with Yahweh (the Hebrew name for God).

The journey from the garden to the city is arduous yet exhilarating as we come face to face with ourselves and our 21st-century lives. On the surface, the primeval world of scripture bears little resemblance to our own, but probing deeper, we find our own challenges are not far removed from those of the ancients. The people we meet in the story travel through life, navigate the complexities of each day, and long for the day when all wrongs will be made right. Like our ancestors, we seek our own solutions to these difficulties and wonder why it doesn't work, or why we cannot just make the jump to the end of the story and enter the promised perfection. This is where hope enters.

We do not walk this journey without the expectant hope that the Advent season brings. Through Advent, we anticipate the arrival of the one who will deal a decisive blow to the enemy and offer humanity the hope it so desperately craves. Genesis 3:15 has been called the *Proto Evangelium* or *First Gospel* because it is the first hint in the story of the one coming who will crush the head of the evil one and restore our relationship with Yahweh.

The hostilities we face on this journey are not battles fought against flesh and blood, but against the seed of the serpent, also known as principalities, powers, and rulers of the darkness. Our struggles are a lived reality of the unseen, cosmic battle of the ages between God and Satan that will ultimately be won through the seed of the woman. This seed will become a child born unto us – Jesus Christ, God incarnate, the Savior of the world. This is the hope that lights the way of the Advent season, the expectant hope that arrives with the one born in Bethlehem. My prayer for you is that this hope will come alive in you and continue to unfold in your hearts as together, we journey to the manger.

Father, as I begin this Advent journey to the manger, reveal the areas in my life where I am striving in my own efforts to navigate the daily struggles and challenges of life. Grant me the grace to slow down during this season and allow the awe, wonder, and expectant hope of Messiah's arrival to fill my heart each day. In Christ's name, amen.

FIRST WEEK OF ADVENT
MONDAY
"THE PROMISE"

Reading: Genesis 12:1-3; 22:1-2, 15-18

And all the nations of the earth will be blessed by your offspring because you have obeyed my command.

GENESIS 22:18 (CSB)

"JUST DO WHAT YOU'RE TOLD!" As a father of five, I have said that countless times to my children, along with this parental gem: "If you would just do what you're told, I would never have to raise my voice, and our coexistence in this house would be peaceful!" Okay, maybe I didn't phrase it exactly like that, but I must admit unquestioned, unchallenged obedience from my children would have made parenting much easier.

The hope of the Advent season is connected to a promise and that promise is anchored in the willing obedience of one man. For reasons we may never understand on this side of eternity, God chose Abraham to be the father of the nation that would bring forth Jesus, the Messiah. Abraham's life is a shining example of faith that we look back on with awe and admiration. His faith was not pie-in-the-sky wishful thinking, but expectant hope, and we are told in Romans when hope was elusive, Abraham's faith rose to the surface.

> He believed, hoping against hope, so that he became
> the father of many nations...Romans 4:18 (CSB)

Faith always requires action and for Abraham, the action required to demonstrate his faith was obedience to God's voice. Twice in his life, he was asked by God to "go." First, in Genesis 12, he was compelled to leave his homeland and go to a place God would show him. Decades later, in Genesis 22, he is again prompted to "go," this time to the land of Moriah where he would offer his son, Isaac, as a sacrifice. In both instances, Abraham was asked to cut ties that held him to earthly things and walk in obedience to gain heavenly promise.

In Genesis 12, he had to cut ties with his past, leaving the comfort and security of home and family to journey to an unknown destination. God said, "if you do this, I will give you a promise, a future hope that all nations of the world will be blessed through you." In this promise, anchored in faith-filled obedience, we see the hope of the Savior foreshadowed, the one whose Kingdom will have no end. (Luke 1:33). In Genesis 22, Abraham had a much more difficult task in cutting ties with his future. Isaac was the promised son through whom the covenant blessing would proceed, and now God asks Abraham to let him go. The patriarch obeyed and with a divine act of love and provision, Yahweh delivered a ram in the thicket for the sacrifice, giving Abraham his son, and his future, back to him.

For some of you, God is calling you to a new level of obedience so He can bring about a promised hope in your life. Maybe it's about releasing things from your past – friends, habits, lifestyles, or painful memories holding you back from following the way of Christ and his best for your life. Cut the ties. For some of you, it's trusting Yahweh with your future. God is nudging you to take your future hopes and dreams and lay them before Him, knowing He alone holds the future and is the source of our provision. Cut the ties. When we are willing to cut ties with our past, God gives us a future. When we are willing to cut ties with our future, God gives hope and a future back to us. Abraham's radical obedience anchors a faith that gives us a promised hope.

Father, I receive your call to radical obedience. My answer to you in all things will simply be "yes." I give you my past for healing, my present for hearing, and my future for walking open-handed in your ways, trusting that you will guide my steps every moment of every day. In Christ's name, amen.

FIRST WEEK OF ADVENT
TUESDAY
"THE SCEPTER"

Reading: Genesis 49:8-12

The scepter will not depart from Judah, Nor the ruler's staff from between his feet, Until Shiloh comes, And to him shall be the obedience of the peoples.

GENESIS 49:10 (NAS)

OUR WORLD IS IN CONSTANT TURMOIL. Great tension exists between nations, groups of nations, political rivals, and social factions. The days of civil discourse and mutual disagreement have, sadly, faded away. "If you aren't with me, you are against me" is the battle cry of our day and social media does nothing but exacerbate the ever-escalating pressure to choose one side and vilify the other. The turmoil without reflects turmoil within as fear, anxiety, depression, anger, greed, and a litany of other emotions dominate the soul of humanity. There is no rest, only constant strife, and endless upheaval.

When Jacob, the son of Isaac and grandson of Abraham, was nearing the end of his life, he brought his 12 sons before him to pronounce blessings and prophesy concerning their future. As Judah stood before his aged father, the pronounced blessing spoke of a "scepter," a royal staff that would be established in his lineage, indicating the line of kingly rule and authority will remain with Judah's descendants forever. According to the prophecy, the climax of Judah's royal lineage would happen when "Shiloh comes" and all the peoples of the earth bow in homage.

Scholars are all over the map when it comes to the meaning of *Shiloh* (pronounced "She-Low"), but most agree Shiloh is the Messiah, the seed of the woman and promised heir of Abraham. "Shiloh" could be translated as "rest" and it speaks of a day when all the peoples of the earth (note the plural) will find rest in this King from the line of Judah who holds the scepter in his hand. The writer of Hebrews confirms the scepter is in the hand of God's only Son.

> But about the Son he says, "Your throne, O God, will last for ever and ever; a scepter of justice will be the scepter of your kingdom. Hebrews 1:8 (CSB)

One might ask, "if Shiloh has come, why is there still turmoil, and why does unrest rule the day?" It's a legitimate question, but God always desires that humanity, out of their own willingness, moves to action. When Shiloh came, He extended this encouragement to all:

> Come to me all of you who are weary and burdened, and I will give you rest. Take up my yoke...and you will find rest for your souls. Matthew 11:28-29 (CSB)

To those mired in the mayhem of this world, be encouraged. If you find yourself weary, burdened, anxious, and fearful, here is an open invitation. Shiloh has come and you are invited to find Him in a manger in Bethlehem. The Lion of the tribe of Judah awaits all who will make the journey and come to find rest in Him.

There is another layer to this as we anticipate the coming of Christ. Our turmoil-stricken world longs for rest and needs to see the rest that Shiloh brings lived out through us, His people. We who understand Jacob's prophecy must enter that rest and live as a non-anxious presence in a world that knows only the opposite. Our culture needs a new narrative, one that refuses the way of discord and dissension and demonstrates a better way, full of the rest that only comes from the one who holds the scepter – Shiloh.

Father, today I bring all my anxiety and lay it before your Son, the Lion of the tribe of Judah who has the scepter in his hand and holds all things together. May the rest Shiloh brings saturate my life and spill over to others as a living example of our Savior's rest. In Christ's name, amen.

FIRST WEEK OF ADVENT
WEDNESDAY
"THE KINGDOM"

Reading: 2 Samuel 7:1-17; Jeremiah 23:3-6

Your house and kingdom will endure before me forever, and
your throne will be established forever.

2 SAMUEL 7:16 (CSB)

CENTURIES HAVE NOW PASSED since the promise of the scepter was given to the lineage of Judah. The 430 years of servitude in Egypt, the miraculous deliverance through the waters of the Red Sea, the wilderness wanderings, the possession of the promised land and the disaster of the era of the Judges paved the way for a king in Israel. It wasn't God's ideal, but the people insisted, and the Creator relented, granting them a king. Saul, the first monarch of Israel, was a tragic figure whose failure opened the door for a young war hero from the line of Judah to ascend to the throne. David, the eighth son of Jesse the Bethlehemite, became Israel's greatest king and despite his many flaws and failures, he is remembered in the legacy of scripture as one who passionately pursued the heart of God. When David's kingdom was established, he experienced *Shi-*

loh, rest from all his enemies, and from that place of rest, he had a burning desire to build a house for the Lord – a temple – a dwelling place. God wasn't interested. Yahweh had something bigger in mind, something to spark the expectant hope of the prophets for generations to come. God flipped the script on David and said, "You aren't going to build a house for me. I am going to build a house for you and this house that I build for you will be established forever. No strings attached."

What we see in this narrative is the scepter prophesied by Jacob moving through the centuries and landing directly in the hand of Judah's descendant, the shepherd King, David. "The Kingdom of Israel's greatest King," God said, "will endure and be established forever." Eight times in 2 Samuel 7, the word "forever" is used as a point of emphasis that the kingdom God is giving to David will have no end. On the surface, it seems like an impossibility. Kingdoms come and go. Kings ascend and fall like the rising and setting of the sun and eventually fade into the annals of history. Yet the covenant promise made by God speaks of an everlasting Kingdom with an everlasting King seated on an everlasting throne.

This fueled the Messianic expectation of God's people, and it serves as a reminder to us that God never forgets a promise. With God, promises made are promises kept, even if it takes what seem like eternity to come to pass. Years down the road, Jeremiah picked up on this promised covenant and declared God will raise up a righteous branch for David who will "reign wisely as king and administer justice and righteousness in the land." (Jer. 23:5)

The expectant hope of Advent not only revolves around the arrival of the King in Bethlehem, but also the return of the King at the end of days to establish the Kingdom as heaven and earth become one. When that day arrives, the scepter of Judah will still be squarely in the hand of the righteous branch who will sit on the throne of David forever. As the Psalmist wrote,

> Your throne, God, is forever and ever; the scepter of your kingdom is a scepter of justice. Psalm 45:6 (CSB)

This is the Kingdom to which we now belong and anticipate its fulfillment with expectant hope.

Father, as I ponder the depth of the promises made to Abraham, Judah, and David, continue to stir hope inside of me. Allow me to walk this journey with patience and an inner security that regards all your promises as "yes and amen." May I hold fast to your Word and never lose hope regardless of what I face. In Christ's name, amen.

FIRST WEEK OF ADVENT
THURSDAY
"THE STUMP"

Reading: Isaiah 6:11-13; 11:1-10

Then a shoot will grow from the stump of Jesse, and a
branch from his roots will bear fruit.

ISAIAH 11:1 (CSB)

ADDICTION, trauma, infidelity, infertility, financial ruin,
unforeseen illness, untimely death... Like angry wind and
waves battering a coastal town, destructive forces have a way
of leaving hopelessness in their wake and etching this question into our minds: "Can anything good come from this?"

In June 2002, two wildfires merged in the east-central
mountains of my home state, Arizona, and became known as
the Rodeo-Chedeski Fire. The fire spread rapidly and burned
for nearly a month, forcing the evacuation of several small,
rural communities. When the fire's last ember was crushed,
more than 460,000 acres of forest had been consumed and
over 400 homes destroyed. I remember driving through the
region shortly after the fire ended and the panoramic view of
the landscape resembled a scene from an apocalypse movie

– devastation, destruction, hopelessness – much like the land-scape of our lives when catastrophic situations hit. Because of Christ's Advent, however, there is always the hope of renewal and restoration of things lost.

Several years later, I drove through the region again and noticed the areas which had been burned by the fire were springing back to life. New trees budded from the ground, fresh grass sprouted from the earth, and the Sitgreaves National Forest was slowly regaining the beauty and splendor lost to the fire. What was once hopeless was now bursting with hope.

When the prophet Isaiah received his calling to ministry, God was straight up with him.

"People won't listen to you. Your message will fall on deaf ears, and it will be a terrible time for my people. Cities will be evacuated and left in ruins. People will be driven to foreign lands and even the ten percent that remains in the land will be burned up. On the surface, there will be no hope. Zero."
(Paraphrase Mine - See Isaiah 6 for the full story)

Sign me up…or not! Can anything good come from this? Then, true to character, God gives a revelation of hope to the prophet.

…like the terebinth or the oak that leaves a stump when felled, the holy seed is in the stump. Isaiah 6:13b (CSB)

Yahweh breathed hope into hopelessness, telling Isaiah that amid the devastation, a seed remained in the land, and from it, life would come. A few chapters later, in today's key reading, we see Isaiah pick up this theme again with a shoot coming from the stump of Jesse because the seed was still there. The holy seed in the stump of the land is our Lord and Savior, the Holy One upon whom hope and salvation rests. In the garden, God established this holy seed that would come through Abraham, Isaac, Jacob, Judah, and David. The seed remained through the centuries and became a righteous branch bringing life to all.

The Arizona forest bloomed again because the seed was in the stump, and because of the holy seed, the Messiah, out of the devastation and destruction of our own lives, hope will rise. Be encouraged: nothing we experience in this life is beyond redemption because the seed is in the stump.

On that day the root of Jesse will stand as a banner for the peoples. The nations will look to him for guidance, and his resting place will be glorious. Isaiah 11:10 (CSB)

Father, as I look at the situations in my life that have brought nothing but devastation and destruction, it is difficult to see any hope. Remind me in those moments there is always hope because of your Son, Jesus. I pray for restoration and renewal in my life, and in the life of my family as I lean into your restorative power. In Christ's name, amen.

FIRST WEEK OF ADVENT
FRIDAY
"THE GOD WHO IS WITH US"

Reading: Isaiah 7:1-17

Therefore, the Lord himself will give you a sign: See, the virgin will conceive, have a son, and name him Immanuel.

ISAIAH 7:14 (CSB)

WITHIN A FEW DECADES of the stump prophecy, the future of the house of David appeared to be in jeopardy. Ahaz, the grandson of King Uzziah, was one of Judah's most wicked monarchs and ruled for sixteen ruinous years in Jerusalem. (See 2 Chronicles 28 for his story). During his administration, Judah fell under the control of a wicked political and military alliance to the north. More than 200,000 of Judah's residents - men, women, and children - were deported, and only the capital city of Jerusalem remained standing. On the surface, all signs pointed to the end of the house of David. Ahaz, along with the remaining inhabitants of Jerusalem, "trembled like trees of a forest shaking in the wind." Isaiah 7:2 (CSB). But as we have seen throughout this first week of Advent, God is always faithful to His promise.

Isaiah and his son were sent by God to lead a clandestine meeting with Ahaz where the prophet let the wicked king know in no uncertain terms, *"...if you do not stand firm in your faith then you will not stand at all.*"– Isaiah 7:9). Ahaz was commanded to dig into his roots and stand firm in God's promise that what had been spoken of his family through the centuries would never fall to the ground. The promised seed established in the house of David will indeed remain.

With a twist of irony, Yahweh seeks to further embed His promise in the heart of the king. He told Ahaz to go ahead and ask for a sign to which the king feigns piety. Isaiah doesn't bend.

"Listen, house of David!" – Isaiah 7:13

What follows not only speaks to Judah's plight, but it also reminds all of us that God never forgets a promise and invites us to anchor our faith in Him. Why? A virgin will have a Son, and name him Immanuel, which means "God with us." We will discuss the virgin birth later in our Advent Journey, but the Hebrew word for *"virgin"* also means *"young woman"* and there is a clear message in the Immanuel prophecy that applies directly to Ahaz, the entire house of David, and ultimately, to us.

For Ahaz, it meant his son, Hezekiah, would reign as a righteous king. So righteous, in fact, it became a sign for the nation that God is with the house of David. That is exactly what happened. For three decades, Hezekiah rebuilt Jerusa-lem, expanded its territory, fortified the military, and gener-ated economic prosperity. He tore down idolatrous altars, re-stored true worship of Yahweh, and spearheaded a revival in the land.

For all humanity, the Immanuel prophecy invites us to re-ceive the virgin-born Son of God as the ultimate fulfillment of "God with us," proving Himself to be forever true and faith-ful. THIS is the faith we must stand firm in. Faith is not just giving mental assent to a set of beliefs. Faith is unwavering trust that stands firm in the truth and places confidence in the unshakable character of God. When I exercise faith, I secure God's truth as the foundation of my thoughts and actions, knowing if my security lay elsewhere, I am left with nothing except shifting sand.

The mandate for Ahaz was simple. Shift your trust and build your foundation on God. He will prove himself to you by being *with* you. It's the same for us. The faithful God who secured the house of David invites us to embrace Immanuel, Christ our Lord, and move from instability to the firm founda-tion established in Him.

Father, forgive me for the times in my life I have doubted you. I pray today for a fresh revelation in my heart of what Immanuel really means. I ask that through this revelation, I will rebuild the foundation of my life on Jesus. I declare with the hymn writer, "On Christ the solid rock I stand. All other ground is shifting sand." In Christ's name, amen.

FIRST WEEK OF ADVENT
SATURDAY
"THE PRINCE OF SHALOM"

Reading: Isaiah 9:1-7

For a child will be born for us, a son will be given to us, and the government will be on his shoulders. He will be named Wonderful Counselor, Mighty God, Eternal Father, Prince of Peace.

ISAIAH 9:6 (CSB)

HOW IS IT WITH YOUR SOUL TODAY? English theologian and evangelist, John Wesley, would often ask this reflective question to those under his watchful care. In modern Christianity, we have adopted a Western, Greek ideal and relegated our souls to being just one compartment of our life along with our body and spirit. Yet in creation, when God breathed His life into Adam, we are told that "man became a living soul" – Genesis 2:7 (KJV). The Hebrew word for "soul" is *nephesh* which is used over 700 times in various ways throughout the Old Testament to describe the essence of who we are. It literally means "that which breathes" and the message is clear that we are a soul because of the life God breathed into us. Created by Him and for Him, we are fully dependent upon Him for the sustenance of life.

Dallas Willard called the soul the "life center of human beings" and it is our soul that integrates our thoughts and actions. When our soul is healthy, drawing its breath from God and allowing His life to be exhaled from us into our relationships and daily activities, we can truly say it is well with our soul. This state of well-being in our soul is what the Bible calls *shalom*. Isaiah prophesied the anticipated Messiah, the child born to bring light to those walking in darkness, will be called the Prince of Shalom – the Prince of Peace who will reign with justice from the throne of David.

Shalom is much more than the absence of conflict or an internal state of serenity. To have shalom is to have well-being in all aspects of life: spiritually, physically, mentally, and emotionally. Living an integrated life free from compartmentalization, whole, and prosperous is to have the shalom of God present and operative within. To invite the Prince of Shalom into our lives is to invite all that we need for our well-being to come to us today.

The journey to the manger involves a quest to find all we need for the well-being of our soul and the Son given to us in Bethlehem is the authority of this well-being. He is the Prince of Shalom, and we must always remember everything we need to live life the way God intended is found only in Him. There is no other name under heaven by which we are saved, and lest we think salvation is only about where we will spend eternity, think again. The one who is called "The Prince of Peace" desires to give our soul a life in Him loaded with well-being for all that we think, say, do, and experience. This has always been the heart of Yahweh for his people. Notice how the blessing of Aaron ends.

> The Lord bless you and keep you; the Lord make his face shine on you and be gracious to you; the Lord turn his face toward you and give you peace (Shalom).
> Numbers 6:24-26 (NIV parentheses added)

Maybe the better question for us would be "Is Shalom ordering your soul today?"

Father, I thank you for always looking out for my well-being. As I reflect on you this day, I bring my disordered soul before you. I ask that your Shalom will permeate my life, bring order to my soul, and allow me to breathe out the same life you have breathed into me. In Christ's name, amen.

SECOND WEEK OF ADVENT
SUNDAY
"THE FEAST"

Reading: Isaiah 25:6-9

"On that day it will be said 'Look, this is our God; we have waited for him, and he has saved us. This is the Lord; we have waited for him. Let us rejoice and be glad in his salvation."

ISAIAH 25:9 (CSB)

IN CENTRAL ARIZONA, 60 miles southeast of Phoenix, lies the historic town of Florence. Founded in 1866, Florence is the sixth oldest non-Native American settlement in the state, boasts a population of roughly 27,000 and has more than 20 buildings listed on the National Historical Registry. It is quite an accomplishment for a small town and yields intense bragging rights among the residents. Another well-known fact is for more than 100 years the state has operated its largest penitentiary in Florence, although recently it was announced the aging prison is to be progressively closed and its inmates relocated to a shiny, new, privately owned facility in a nearby town.

For our family, however, the town of Florence will always hold a special place in our hearts, not because of the historic buildings or, thankfully, the sprawling acres that make up the state prison complex. It is an endearing place for us because of a winery and a wedding feast.

Established in 1906 as Arizona's first brickyard and later a dairy farm, the scenic Windmill Winery offers a distant, but picturesque view of the legendary Superstition Mountains, a lush vineyard, and its own unique label of assorted Arizona-produced wines. Comfortably situated at the north end of the Florence town limits, the Windmill is also an award-winning wedding venue with a serene outdoor courtyard for couples to say their nuptial vows and two options for the newlyweds to party with their families and friends. One is the stunning Lake House and the other, the Big Barn, a classic red farm edifice which was moved piece by piece from Green Bay, Wisconsin when the Winery commenced wedding hosting in 2010. It is a breathtaking location for such a big day.

In 2015, our oldest daughter, Cayla, and her fiancé, Drew, chose the courtyard and Big Barn at the Winery to unite in matrimony on a pleasant December day. All the hard work and preparation was worth it, and we relished every moment of both the wedding and the feast as God miraculously took a bride and groom and made them one flesh.

It is no coincidence that the climax of God's redemptive story for humanity happens at a wedding feast. John the Revelator had a glorious vision of history's climactic moment.

> Let us be glad and rejoice and give him glory, because the marriage of the Lamb has come and the bride has prepared herself.... Blessed are those invited to the marriage feast of the Lamb... Revelation 19:7, 9 (CSB)

John goes on to describe the final defeat of God's enemies and the apex moment where Christ and His bride become one, heaven and earth are joined, and all is made right.

Isaiah sees this moment as a feast of prime cuts of meat and aged wine where the shroud of death that has hung over humanity from the beginning of time is forever destroyed and all tears are wiped away from every face. But notice this: Twice, Isaiah says "we have waited for him." That is the message of Advent. We, the bride, wait with anticipation for the wedding feast where we will be joined with Christ for eternity. As we wait, we enjoy the fine, aged wine of the Holy Spirit who is the guarantee in our hearts of that final redemptive moment. All the challenges we face and all our preparation for His coming will ultimately be worth it. Wine and wedding feasts – Rejoice and be Glad!

Father, I fully anticipate your coming! Thank you for the promise you have given of completing your redemptive work. I accept your invitation to the wedding feast and ask that you fill me with the wine of your Spirit that I may patiently await your arrival with rejoicing and gladness in my heart. In Christ's name, amen.

Reading: Isaiah 35:1-10

"A road will be there and a way; it will be called the Holy Way. The unclean will not travel on it, but it will be for the one who walks the path. Fools will not wander on it."

ISAIAH 35:8 (CSB)

"IT'S MY WAY OR THE HIGHWAY…!" Fortunately, the prophet waxes much more poetic than that. If you haven't noticed in our journey through Isaiah, much of his prophetic work is expressed in poetry. With vivid description and freedom of expression, Isaiah masterfully engages his God-given imagination to paint beautiful portraits of the realities of God and the experiences of his people. Isaiah 35 is one of the prophet's finest works of art as he reaches back to Israel's Exodus story and weaves a colorful tapestry of what life will be like under the banner of the anticipated Messiah.

After the miraculous Red Sea deliverance, Israel faced a harsh and brutal wilderness. Because of God's faithfulness and promise, however, the desert bloomed and provided what the chosen nation needed for its journey toward the promised land. When Israel only saw the barrenness of the wasteland and day-to-day existence became a grinding struggle, God strengthened their weak hands and fortified their shaky knees, thus, providing the persistence they needed to continue. Israel experienced continuous renewal in the wilderness from the hand of its Creator. Isaiah says they were able to…

See when blinded by circumstance,
Hear when the noise of life cluttered the atmosphere,
Leap when their feet felt like the bricks of Egypt, and…
Sing when their tongues were loosened under intense distress.

The high point of this poem speaks of a road for the pilgrims to travel called "the Holy Way." It is holy because it is set apart, different, and like nothing else. Other scriptures refer to it as a "high-way" because it is exactly that – a way that stands high above the well-traveled thoroughfares of humanity. For the Exodus pilgrims, it was a highway of Tabernacle worship and Torah observance. Then, when Christ came and fulfilled all things, He declared *"I am the way… "* – John 14:6 (CSB), making it clear the path of the righteous only travels through Him.

The way of Jesus stands high above the ways of the world and is designed to look different. It is not always an easier way to travel, but it is a better way, and as we travel His way, it serves as a living testimony for all that there is…

A better way to live.

A better way to engage in relationships.

A better way to model marriage.

A better way to express sexuality.

A better way to handle money.

A better way to way to conduct business.

A better way to create beauty and wonder in the world.

Much like the Exodus pilgrims, our own pilgrimage will be fraught with challenges, and the wilderness before us will appear at times to be unrelenting and void of life. But true to character, God provides a promise for the ransomed who choose the Holy Way. Walking in the Holy Way of the Messiah ultimately leads to Zion, the perfection of God. There, in Zion, the redeemed of the Lord will be completely overtaken by joy and gladness and witness the flight of all sorrow and sighing. In this case, His way *IS* the highway.

Father, today I thank you that even in desolate places, you have provided a highway for me to walk in. I declare today that your Son, Jesus, is the way and I choose to walk in the path He has laid before me. Strengthen my hands when my work becomes weary and my knees when walking the way becomes difficult. With great anticipation, I look forward to Zion and your glorious perfection. In Christ's name, amen.

SECOND WEEK OF ADVENT
TUESDAY
"THE VOICE (PART 1)"

Reading: Isaiah 40:1-2

"Comfort, comfort my people," says your God."

ISAIAH 40:1 (CSB)

ABOUT 100 YEARS AFTER the life and ministry of Isaiah, the Babylonian army besieged Jerusalem. The besieging turned into invasion and, ultimately, thousands of Hebrews were carted off to the capital city of the empire where they spent the next 70 years in exile. The Babylonian Exile, as it is known, became forever etched into the collective memory of Israel as it ended their nation, priesthood, and temple. On the surface, it appeared Yahweh was dead and Marduk, the chief god of the Babylonians, had won.

The Exile was a mess of their own making. Repeatedly throughout the centuries, prophetic voices like those of Isaiah and Jeremiah thundered their warnings to the people of God. "Repent, or you will bring disaster upon yourselves," was the message, but Judah ignored the warnings, served other gods, lived contrary to the ways of Yahweh, and ultimately paid the price. For two generations in Babylon, the Hebrews lived with the reality of what wasn't, the loss of what was, and the regret of what could have been.

Maybe this is a microcosm of your life right now. You lie in a bed of your own doing and regret surrounds you. A dark pall hangs over your soul and a sense of abandonment casts a shadow over your life. What was once there exists no more. The nearness of God's presence and the sound of His tender voice calling were staples for you, but a little sin here, a few bad decisions there, ignoring spiritual practices and community with God's people – and it all slipped away.

Maybe you are on a different spectrum. Perhaps it is well in your own life, but you see the world jumping off the rails. Those you love are teetering on the brink of destruction. You have tried like Isaiah to be a prophetic voice, but the spoken words have fallen on deaf ears, and what you feared the most came upon their lives: despair…exile…failure.

Then, out of nowhere, a voice thunders – clear, loving, powerful, and full of hope. "Comfort, comfort my people!" declares Yahweh. The voice that spoke the universe into existence and brought order from chaos in the creation now speaks, reminding us we are not abandoned, and the relationship we have with Him still exists. This is *your* God speaking. The one who loved you from the beginning and brought you out of exile in Egypt is also bringing you out of exile in Babylon. Despite everything, He is still your God, and He speaks "comfort" – twice.

This important Hebrew word for "comfort" declares that God feels the pain of His people and sends this message of hope because He shares their agony. He is not an aloof deity waiting to pour out His wrath and say, *"I told you so."* He is moved with compassion and drawn to us, longing to see heartache and brokenness restored to health and wholeness. This is exactly what Christ came to do – to share in our agony and draw us from our exile back into a vibrant relationship with Him.

Yahweh speaking over an oppressed people foreshadows the coming Messiah whose voice will preach good news to the poor and proclaim freedom for those held captive. Hear the voice speak today. He speaks tenderly, "your time of exile is over, and your iniquity is pardoned." *That* is reason to rejoice.

Father, in a noisy world, allow me to hear your voice above all. I long to hear you speak, for when you speak you create new things. My life needs the tangible reality of your presence, especially in those seasons when I stray from you. My ear is attentive, and I stand ready for words of comfort and change. Speak, Lord, I pray. In Christ's name, amen.

SECOND WEEK OF ADVENT
WEDNESDAY
"THE VOICE (PART 2)"

Reading: Isaiah 40:3-5

"A voice of one crying out: Prepare the way of the Lord in the wilderness; make a straight highway for our God in the desert."

ISAIAH 40:3 (CSB)

"OKAY, KIDS, WE NEED TO DO A 10-MINUTE TIDY." The 10-minute tidy was my wife's brainchild, and I am sure most families have some version of it. For us, this was simple: pick up all the trash, empty and reload the dishwasher, run the vacuum, relocate the clothes from the common areas to the bedrooms, wipe down the counters, spray the room freshener, light a few candles, and 'voila'! The appearance of a clean house. With five kids at home, the 10-minute tidy usually went smoothly. On the happen-chance that an unexpected guest dropped by, we were prepared. The guest could enter the home, look around, and think, "wow, they have five kids and keep such a beautiful home." Little did they know if a bedroom door opened, an avalanche would take place.

There is a vast difference between a 10-minute tidy and

diligently preparing for the arrival of a guest. With advance notice, the scene would look entirely different. Preparing the way for a guest would involve scrubbing of baseboards, washing of walls, arranging of rooms, clothes hung up or placed in drawers, steaming the carpets, organizing the pantry, cleaning the windows, sweeping the patio, and manicuring the yards – all with great attention to detail.

On the heels of the voice of comfort, Isaiah describes another voice calling out to Yahweh's people. This voice comes from the wilderness and invites them to prepare the way for the arrival of the Lord. "He is coming," declares the voice, and the way needs to be made straight, free from all obstacles. Creating a straight path is challenging and involves significant work. Mountains don't self-level. Bends in the highway don't become straight without substantial reconstruction efforts. Rough roads don't become smooth without removal of obstructions and consistent grading.

The question we must answer this Advent season is "how are we preparing for the arrival of the Lord?" Are we taking the 10-minute tidy approach, praying the Lord does not open the rooms of our life we want to remain hidden? Or will we go to work and level some mountains and straighten some crooked places while laboring to smooth out the rough patches?

The beauty of this kind of preparation is we don't have to do it alone. Often, we need direction. When our family was in full-blown preparation mode, my wife provided much-needed direction because inevitably the kids and I would miss things.

Gwen's God-given gift for details made the process easier and more thorough. We are told in Proverbs:

> Trust in the Lord with all your heart and lean not on your own understanding; in all your ways submit to him, and he will make your paths straight.
> Proverbs 3:5-6 (NIV)

Preparing the way is really a partnership between us and our Creator. We fully trust and submit to Him, and He shows us how to clean, reconstruct, reroute and re-grade our lives so that when He comes, we are truly prepared. We who anticipate His coming listen to the voice and concentrate on the preparation. A 10-minute tidy won't get the job done.

Father, as we anticipate your coming, may we always make diligent preparation. Give us the eyes to always trust and acknowledge you, knowing we are never alone. Give us the ears to hear your voice calling us and directing us in how to make changes in our lives that will ultimately reveal your glory to the world. In Christ's name, amen.

Reading: Isaiah 42:1-9

"A bruised reed He will not break and a dimly burning wick He will not extinguish; He will faithfully bring forth justice."

ISAIAH 42:3 (NAS)

"I DON'T WANT REVENGE, I WANT JUSTICE!" Such is the cry of those who have been wounded by others or damaged by oppressive systems that thrive on favoritism and domination. In our world, when we speak of justice, what we really want is fairness, an impartial system based on well-reasoned arguments to decide what is right. In the end, if there has been a wrong, we believe somebody must pay for what was done. Only then will justice have been served. The problem is our justice system is subjective. Justice for one does not always mean justice for all because inevitably, a person or a group of persons decide what justice is and how it should be dispensed. In the end, someone will be left angry and unsatisfied leading to an endless cycle of seeking retribution.

Isaiah 42 marks the first of four "servant songs," poetic

frames to introduce God's chosen servant, the Messiah, to the world. Here, the servant is described as one walking in the power of the Spirit who will unassumingly bring justice to the nations. We are told this servant will not rest until justice is established and made foundational. Biblical justice brought by the servant is not the blindfolded lady with a scale in her hand. According to Yahweh, justice is the exercise of righteousness. It is the full expression of the character of God revealed on the earth. Justice is complete adherence to God's ways, and it is the one called "my servant," the Messiah, who will bring it to pass.

When the servant brings God's justice to the Earth, there is a special heart for the broken, bruised, and marginalized for he will not "break a reed that is bruised or put out a smoldering wick." With God's servant at the helm, there is no situation beyond repair, and no matter how close to extinction one seems, the servant heals the bruised and wounded, and fans back into flame the hope that was lost.

There is an aspect of God's justice that cannot be ignored, however. The execution of righteousness and expression of God's character falls squarely on the shoulders of all who have come under the care of the servant. He says to us:

"…I will watch over **you**, and I will appoint **you**…to open blind eyes, to bring out prisoners from the dungeon, and those sitting in darkness from the prison house…"
Isaiah 42:6-7 (CSB) (emphasis added)

We who have embraced Christ, the faithful servant of Yahweh, bear His name on the Earth; and if we live under His righteousness and character, we have the responsibility to dispense what we have received from Him – justice. The bruised reeds and smoldering wicks we see and encounter every day need a revelation of God's love that goes beyond ourselves. So many people are waiting this Advent season for the arrival of something new in their lives that will restore hope and we who carry the hope are obligated to give it back out.

"Do justice, love mercy" – Micah 6:8, is what is required because Christ arrives through us to the people of this world. The next time we hear the cries for justice, let us remember not only the servant who established it but also the challenge to us to deliver it.

Father, I thank you for operating under a different system of justice than the world does, and I am grateful you have shown us your character. Remind me, Lord, that you have called me to look for the bruised reeds and smoldering wicks of this world to give a demonstration of your mercy and justice. In Christ's name, amen.

SECOND WEEK OF ADVENT
FRIDAY
"THE LIGHT"

Reading: Isaiah 49:1-7

"...It is not enough for you to be my servant raising up the tribes of Jacob and restoring the protected ones of Israel. I will also make you a light for the nations, to be my salvation to the ends of the earth."

ISAIAH 49:6 (CSB)

"THIS LITTLE LIGHT OF MINE, I'm gonna let it shine, let it shine, let it shine, let it shine..." is one of the great Sunday school refrains of the ages. With a simple melody and catchy rhythm, it has become more than just a kids' song. Gospel choirs and congregations alike have worshiped to it, with hand motions included. It is one of those songs that will probably never die. Isaiah's second servant song is ultimately about this light, which is anything but little.

Walking through Advent's grand story, we have seen that it all started with the promise of a seed that was to come through Abraham, his sons, and eventually, the nation of Israel. Israel was called to reflect God's glory in the Earth and demonstrate to the other nations of the world what life under the banner of Yahweh can be – inviting and fulfilling. Repeatedly, Israel left the covering of the one who called, rescued, and formed them, but Yahweh never went back on his promise or reneged on His covenants with Abraham and David. The promise of a Savior to shine a light to lead Israel from its self-imposed darkness will come, according to Isaiah, through this one called "the servant."

The servant, pointing to Christ the Messiah, is called by Yahweh. He is named in the womb of his mother and filled with the words of His heavenly Father which pierce like a sharpened arrow. He is formed to be a servant and called to bring Israel back to its Creator, but in an interesting twist, Yahweh declares, "it is not enough." The mission the servant is called to will expand beyond the children of Abraham because, ultimately, Yahweh desires all of humanity to be saved. The servant, therefore, will become "...a light for all nations to be my salvation to the ends of the earth."

When Jesus, the servant, was in the world, He declared that His Father's house was to be a house for all nations (Isaiah 56:7; Mark 11:17). This was a passion of our Lord, so much that when He witnessed the nations being restricted from coming to the house to experience God, He turned over the tables and drove out all who hindered.

The servant has now passed his mission of being the light to the nations on to his followers.

"Go, therefore, and make disciples of all nations... teaching them to observe everything I have commanded you."
Matthew 28:19 (CSB)

This is the mandate we have inherited. Yesterday, we saw our task is to dispense justice and mercy. Today we see that just as He came as the light of the world to the nations, we carry the mantle of the Servant to be the unhidden city on the hill that demonstrates by our good works the glory of our redeemer. We don't hide this light that burns in our heart under a bushel...NO! We let it shine, brightly. A dark world desperately needs a homing beacon to lead the way for the nations. This is the seed. This is Israel. This is the Servant-Messiah. This is us. Let it shine!

"Father, our world spins in darkness, but you have provided the light through your Servant. This is the light that shines in our hearts, and we accept the mantle of the Servant to shine His light, now our light, into our world. We will not hide it or allow it to be extinguished. Give us your grace to beam it brightly. In Christ's name, amen.

SECOND WEEK OF ADVENT
SATURDAY
"THE FACE"

Reading: Isaiah 50:4-10

"The Lord God will help me; therefore I have not been humiliated; therefore I have set my face like flint, and I know I will not be put to shame."

ISAIAH 50:7 (CSB)

I REMEMBER IT VIVIDLY. It was the last night of summer church camp, 1981. Two weeks shy of my 13th birthday, I sensed God calling me into ministry. There was no lightning bolt from heaven or angelic choir singing in the background, but I knew I heard His voice clearly. That night I said "yes" and made a commitment to Christ that I would do whatever He wanted. It was simple and sincere, but honestly, I have not always been great at walking it out. Following Christ's calling may be the best life, but it is far from the easiest life, and like so many, I am prone to seek out what is easy rather than what is required.

The third servant song shows us one who is willing to do whatever it takes to fulfill the mission, even if it means personal discomfort, opposition, and suffering. Western culture is averse to these things. We seek a journey of ease, comfort, and safety, free from adversity, but the servant demonstrates only one thing matters – doing what He was called to do. The Anticipated One boldly proclaimed His purpose was not to do His own will, but the will of His Father (John 6:38). To establish justice and provide light to the nations ultimately required of the servant a resolve that sought no shortcuts.

In this song, we see one who is teachable and speaks what he has learned, whose knowledge comes from a finely tuned hearing ear. The servant is neither self-seeking nor rebellious, but rather, humbled and yielded. In the face of severe opposition, there is no retreat – only resolve. One translation of our key verse reads:

"Because the Sovereign Lord helps me, I will not be disgraced. Therefore, I have set my face like a stone, determined to do his will. And I know I will not be put to shame." Isaiah 50:7 (NLT)

Luke's Gospel records that when it was time for the Servant's purpose to be fulfilled, he "set his face to go to Jerusalem." – Luke 9:51 (ESV). Setting the face like a stone of flint requires an inner determination that will not buckle or bend under pressure. Knowing what was ahead, Jesus went to Jerusalem. Mocking, beating, and suffering lay ahead but His commitment to the will of the Father was firm.

Flint is a sedimentary rock known for hardness and strength. The Judean Wilderness is loaded with flint, and it is no coincidence Jesus faced the deepest testing of His life in that same wilderness. We can visualize Christ in the wilderness being tempted by Satan to take the stones of flint and turn them to bread. We can see Him recalling these words of Isaiah and in the fire of enemy opposition, being filled with resolve. "No. I will be the bread of life. I am God's word made flesh and I will show humanity what it looks like to do God's will in the face of temptation and hostility." When the Servant returned from the wilderness full of God's spirit, He possessed the inner strength like flint that would carry Him through His ministry and allow Him to set his face toward the cross.

When we see the Servant in this light, we are challenged to stop looking for easy roads out of difficult situations. In the face of opposition, we must dig deep and find a determination like a stone of flint forged in the wilderness. We must stay teachable and stand in a posture of listening to His voice while practicing his presence. Only then will we find the resolve to follow the calling we said "yes" to.

Father, there have been countless times I have taken the easy road and missed out on your plans for my life. I invite you to take me back to the wilderness where I can learn once again what it means to rely on you and hear your voice. While there, build in me a resolve to do your will in times of triumph and times of adversity. In Christ's name, amen.

Reading: Isaiah 52:13-53:9

"See, my servant will be successful; he will be raised and lifted up and greatly exalted."

ISAIAH 52:13 (CSB)

SUCCESS IS _____. You fill in the blank. The dictionary definition of success is simply "reaching a goal," but our culture defines it much more subjectively. Some, like motivational speaker, Tony Robbins, define it in epicurean terms.

"...Success is to live your life in a way that causes you to feel a ton of pleasure, and very little pain."

Secretary of State Colin Powell was more stoic.

"Success is the result of perfection, hard work, learning from failure, loyalty, and persistence."

One of my personal favorites comes from Booker T. Washington.

"Success is to be measured not so much by the position that one has reached in life as by the obstacles which he has overcome."

The fourth servant song begins with a declaration from Yahweh that His servant will be successful. Some translations read he will "prosper." If we stop right there, we are in good company. When Christ was born, there was indeed a Messianic anticipation among Israel. They anticipated the success of their Messiah to be based on being a conquering king, one who would overthrow the tyranny of Roman occupation and restore the throne of David to Israel. What they did not expect with the Advent of Messiah was the rest of Isaiah's fourth servant song.

The third song teases what the fourth song expounds on: the servant will be successful in his mission to establish justice and bring the light of salvation to the nations because he suffers. The first Christians, reading Isaiah through fresh eyes, knew this spoke of Christ. They knew that He, being raised up and exalted, had nothing to do with becoming a conquering war hero and everything to do with His suffering, death, burial, and resurrection.

The hint of physical beating in the third song came to full realization here in the fourth song as the servant is marred and disfigured to the point of no longer resembling a human. He is not a desirable person, in fact, he is despised, rejected, devalued, and marginalized by the very ones he came to save. With his suffering, he becomes one who bears sickness and carries the pain of others. He is pierced, crushed, and punished because of us – sheep gone astray from Yahweh seeking to work out life on our own terms.

When wrongly accused, like a lamb facing shearing and slaughter, the servant is silent; and when he dies, he is buried in a borrowed rich man's tomb. Yet, the servant is considered successful. The first followers of Jesus were fully convinced their Messiah had indeed arrived. The anticipated one had come and through His suffering and death, He became salvation for all people. The servant did for us what we could not do for ourselves and though we deserved nothing, He elevated us to renewed relationship with God. He was raised up on a cross and exalted on high to make a way for us to be raised together with Him in heavenly places. *That* is a successful servant.

Perhaps we should adopt this definition: "Success is giving of yourself and suffering on behalf of others so they can be raised up."

Father, I am indeed grateful that you suffered on my behalf to restore me to the right relationship with you. Through your Son, I see how wrongly we have defined success in our world. Allow me to follow his example, seek success your way and be willing to give of myself to those far from you so they can see your love in me. In Christ's name, amen.

Reading: Isaiah 53:10-12

"...he willingly submitted to death, and was counted among the rebels; yet he bore the sin of many and interceded for the rebels."

ISAIAH 53:12 (CSB)

YANKEE AND REBEL — the names of two German Shepherd dogs that belonged to my childhood friends who lived across the street. From what I can recall, they were docile animals, easy to be around. I didn't understand the significance of the names until later in elementary school when we studied the American Civil War. The soldiers fighting for the Union Army in the north were the "Yankees." The Confederate soldiers fighting in the south were the "Rebels" who broke from the relationship with the Union, casting aside century-old alliances. Refusing to live under the authority of the United States and its governing leaders, the Rebels seceded from the Union and made war with the Yankees. The result was death.

Before we turn this into a history lesson, let's take this metaphor and bring it to the fourth servant song. The anticipated Messiah's coming dismantled the box containing Israel's Messianic hopes. Nobody anticipated a suffering servant. Nobody anticipated one who would be killed by our sins and certainly, nobody anticipated that the long-awaited King would be counted among the rebels.

Rebels in a biblical sense are transgressors who have broken the covenant with Yahweh and refused to live under His authority. Rebels refuse to follow God's way, preferring to chart their own course and do as they please. Rebellion is continuing this path while remaining fully aware God wants humanity to live according to *His* way. Even still, the servant arrives in Bethlehem and ends up at Golgotha, crucified between thieves, counted among the rebels. In the presence of His disciples just hours before his arrest, trial, and execution, Jesus spoke of himself, quoting Isaiah 53.

> "...For the time has come for this prophecy about me to be fulfilled: 'He was counted among the rebels...' "
> Luke 22:37 (NLT)

The righteous rebel servant justified us by carrying our rebellious sin to the cross and bearing it upon Himself as He willingly gave up His life to purge our sin and conquer death. This is the fascinating paradox seen in the fourth song: He willingly gave up his life, but we, the rebels, killed him. He was...

> Rejected by *us,*
> *We* turned away from him,
> *We* devalued him,
> He bore *our* sickness,
> He carried *our* pain.

Then we, the rebellious ones, looked at the suffering servant as being struck down by Yahweh, smitten and afflicted by the Creator. But the one counted among the rebels fulfilled on the cross what had been promised from the garden through the prophets. Paul brilliantly declared what was happening.

> "...That is, in Christ, God was reconciling the world to himself, not counting their trespasses against them..."
> 2 Corinthians 5:19 (CSB)

The suffering servant, counted among the rebels, bore our rebellion and through that selfless act, all of God's rebels are now welcomed home, forgiven, and made whole. This story must be told and there is no better time of the year to tell it than now. Even though the work on the cross was complete, we anticipate the wonder of Christ coming to all the rebels of our generation and unveiling the truth that the Messiah died the death we deserved to die so we could live the life we don't deserve to live.

Father, you were under no obligation to send your Son to be counted among rebels like myself. Forgive me for the times I have charted my own course and failed to follow your life-giving ways. I am grateful that the suffering servant did for me what I could not do for myself and reconciled my relationship with you. I praise you for this today! In Christ's name, amen.

THIRD WEEK OF ADVENT
TUESDAY
"THE FORGIVER"

Reading: Isaiah 55:1-13

Let the wicked one abandon his way and the sinful one his thoughts; let him return to the Lord, so he may have compassion on him, and to our God, for he will freely forgive.

ISAIAH 55:7 (CSB)

HOLDING A GRUDGE CAN BE TOXIC. My maternal grandparents were good people at their core, but they held grudges against those who had wronged them. As a young boy, I listened to them air their grievances, unpacking in detail what was done and why those who wronged them were terrible people. The older I got, the worse it got, and when my birth mom died from cancer in 1992 (I was 23), for reasons unknown my grandparents blamed my dad and, ultimately, God for mom's death. They lived 12 more years wallowing in unforgiveness, holding grudges and I watched it slowly rob them of their life, energy, and health.

Isaiah 55 is an invitation into a new world. The servant who arrived to establish justice and be Yahweh's salvation to the ends of the Earth says to the thirsty ones: "Come!" The covenant made with David has been fulfilled and we are invited to enter the fullness of what the King brought: provision, citizenship in this new world, and an opportunity to be a bastion of hope for the nations.

In the middle of this incredible poem, Isaiah restates familiar themes we have seen in our Advent journey. The thirsty ones are urged to seek Yahweh, abandon all contrary ways, and return because we have a God who will freely forgive. The good news is, Yahweh does not hold a grudge against humanity for past sins and failures. He isn't perched in the heavens talking trash about us to the angels, anxious to smite us with His wrath. He wants us to come to Him so He can forgive us abundantly.

Perhaps the most quoted section of Isaiah 55 proclaims God's ways and thoughts are not ours, in fact, they are higher. "Thoughts," however, do not speak of our Creator's rational superiority. That is a given. He is God. We are not. "Thoughts" in the Hebrew worldview have nothing to do with reason and everything to do with the unexplainable mercy of God. Yahweh forgives and that is where His thoughts, intentions, and purposes for us lie. God's intention and purpose for the thirsty ones is to forgive and those powerful words, "I forgive you" do not return void, but they accomplish the purpose for which they were sent — forgiveness, wholeness, and healing.

This is what we are invited into. Come to the priceless waters of mercy and forgiveness, and then demonstrate the same. Don't be a grudge holder and allow it to rot your bones.

Be a forgiver like our servant Messiah and as Isaiah declares, "you will go out with great joy."

Months before my grandmother passed away, she lived with our family for a short season. One evening, my dad came by the house unannounced, and we had no idea how it was going to go. After a few minutes of visiting with dad, we heard grandma with her walker coming down the hallway and we braced for the worst, as she and dad had barely spoken for the past 12 years. Much to our shock, we had a wonderful visit together as a family and after dad left, grandma said these powerful words to my wife and me in her thick, Kentucky drawl: "You know, I figure that it's best to forgive and let bygones be bygones." Her final months with us were amazing and I saw, even for a moment, her joy return. She finished her race with joy, all because of forgiveness.

Father, thank you for your mercy and forgiveness shown to me. Search my heart today, Lord, and reveal to me where I have held grudges and harbored bitterness in my heart against people. Let me walk in your grace to extend your forgiveness to those in my life who have wronged me, that I may go forth in life with great joy. In Christ's name, amen.

Reading: Isaiah 61:1-11

THE TOWN OF NAZARETH where Jesus spent his early years lies in the Lower Galilee region along a mountainous ridge and is currently the largest city in Northern Israel with a population of about 80,000. Mt. Precipice, on the southern edge of the ridge offers a stunning panoramic view of the lush Jezreel Valley where numerous Old Testament stories took place and much of Israel's history was shaped. Mt. Precipice is also the traditional site of a pivotal moment recorded in Luke 4:28-29 when the residents of the tiny village became so enraged by Jesus's claims, they brought Him to the edge of a cliff with the intent to hurl Him to His death.

Moments earlier, in the local synagogue, Jesus was handed the scroll of Isaiah, opened it, and read these words:

"The Spirit of the Lord God is on me because the Lord has anointed me to bring good news..." Isaiah 61:1 (CSB)

He continued reading to the crowd about this good news changing lives and hastening a day of Jubilee for all humanity. Then, Jesus made a startling statement as all eyes in the synagogue were fastened on Him. "Today, as you listen, this scripture has been fulfilled."– Luke 4:21 (CSB)

In that moment, Jesus effectively announced His arrival as the long-awaited Messiah prophesied throughout scripture. The word *Messiah* in Hebrew means *Anointed One* and here in the Nazareth synagogue, Jesus assumed this title. Today, right here, right now, the Messianic expectation of the ages is being fulfilled. In a small town like Nazareth which had maybe 200 residents in the first century, everybody knew everybody, and upon hearing these words, the crowd in the synagogue paused. "Wait a second...this is Joseph's son?" they whispered. "He's the carpenter's kid. He can't be the Anointed One!"

The claim itself didn't send the gathering into a frenzy. Jesus, using Old Testament examples, let them know the good news — the liberty, restoration, and renewal that the anointed one brings — will be for all humanity, not just the Jewish people. He made it clear if the people of Nazareth could not accept the gospel being for all nations, they could not receive it for themselves. That is what sent them over the edge. The gospel proclamation in Isaiah 61 is rich as the Messiah brings good news to the poor, heals the broken hearted, proclaims freedom to captives and prisoners, comforts those who mourn and trades ashes of destruction for wondrous beauty.

But let us not miss this: It is the desire of the Anointed One to plant us like righteous trees and give us the stability in our lives we need to continue Messiah's work in our generation. We are the ones who rebuild ancient ruins, restore former devastations, and bring renewal to ruined cities. The anticipated ministry of the Anointed One becomes our ministry. It won't always make us popular among the residents of the world, and it might get us thrown off a cliff, but as God's Spirit rested upon Jesus, the Messiah, it rests upon us. We need not fear. We simply go forth and proclaim the good news of the Anointed One.

Father, I am humbled that you would include me in your mission. This is not something I take lightly. Allow my life to be firmly planted in you so that when pressure comes on this mission, I will not waver, but stand strong. I realize the gospel message is foolishness to some, and I am prepared for adversity. Let your Holy Spirit rest on me and anoint me for the task at hand. In Christ's name, amen.

THIRD WEEK OF ADVENT
THURSDAY
"THE ASH HEAP"

Reading: Micah 5:2-5a

"But you, Bethlehem Ephrathah, though you are small among the clans of Judah, out of you will come for me one who will be ruler over Israel, whose origins are from of old, from ancient times."

MICAH 5:2 (NIV)

IN MANY WAYS, the prophecies relating to Advent are like a mosaic work of art. Mosaics utilize small, colored pieces of glass, ceramic, or stone that, when assembled, create the image. Likewise, the ancient prophecies, each with its own unique color and texture, when constructed, create for us a beautiful portrait of the Messiah. Moses contributes, as do the Psalmists, the writer of Samuel, and Isaiah. 700 years before the birth of Jesus, the prophet Micah, a contemporary of Isaiah, adds his unique piece to the mosaic of Christ. Using poetic language in the manner of his contemporaries, Micah knew that exile was coming for Judah, but he also knew something else. He knew where the Messiah was to be born – Bethlehem. But not just Bethlehem – "Bethlehem Ephrathah" and out of this beautiful poem, Micah will let us know that hope is found in the least likely places.

We first encounter Bethlehem when Rachel, the favorite wife of Jacob, dies while giving birth to her second son, Benjamin. We are told that...

> "...she was buried on the way to Ephrath (that is Bethlehem)."
> Gen. 35:19 (ESV)

One of the meanings of *Ephrathah* is "ash heap" and Micah declares the one who will rule Israel and shepherd the people in the strength of the Lord will be born next to the ash heap. What an incredible picture of the gospel! The Messiah will be born next door to a place of great sorrow to bring about great hope. Hope is often found in the least likely places. An ash heap can represent our hopes and dreams burned up and reduced to a smoldering pile of nothing.

You were on a great path toward retirement and a market crash wiped it all out.

You dreamed of having a child, but infertility has plagued you.

You wanted to buy a house, but inflation hit, and interest rates skyrocketed.

You planned to travel the world and then your spouse got the unexpected medical report, and their life was cut short.

Your dreams of being promoted in your company turned to dust when you were passed over for someone less qualified despite your great track record.

In these situations, and so many more, your perspective says there is no hope and all you can see in front of you is an ash heap. But we cannot be afraid to wait with expectancy by the ash heap because hope is often found in the least likely places. If we wait long enough, we might just find our way into a cave and come face to face with God lying in a manger. Coming face to face with God amid the ash heap of our life will change us, because in the manger in Ephrathah lies the one who is willing to take our ashes and give us something more beautiful than we could have ever thought possible. The Psalmist reminds us that...

> "He raises the poor from the dust and lifts the needy from the ash heap." Psalm 113:7 (NIV)

Ephrathah has another meaning – "fruitful." This is ultimately our hope, that the one born by the ash heap can turn it all around and bring about something fruitful. Hope is indeed found in the least likely places. Wait for it. As the song of the season says of Bethlehem, "the hopes and fears of all the years are met in thee tonight."

Father, so many times I have experienced shattered dreams in this broken world. But you have a way of taking the broken pieces of my life and fitting them together into something beautiful. The things I face right now may discourage me,

*but I refuse to lose hope, for I know you are coming to meet
me next to the ash heap. In Christ's name, amen.*

———————————————

THIRD WEEK OF ADVENT
FRIDAY
"THE BOOK"

Reading: Matthew 1:1-17

The book of the generation of Jesus Christ, the son of David, the son of Abraham.

MATTHEW 1:1 (KJV)

AFTER AN INCREDIBLE JOURNEY through Old Testament prophecies regarding the advent of the Messiah, we now turn our attention to the stories in the New Testament surrounding the birth of Jesus. Matthew opens his Gospel with three sets of fourteen genealogies walking us through the earthly lineage of Christ – fourteen from Abraham to David; fourteen from David to the exile; and fourteen from the exile to the birth of Christ. It seems like an odd and rather cumbersome way to begin a story, but to grasp the significance of this passage, we need to understand some basics.

Matthew was one of 12 men called by Jesus to be his closest disciples. As a Jew, Matthew was steeped in the ways of Torah and when he penned his account of the life of Christ, his primary purpose was to convince Jewish readers that Jesus of

Nazareth was indeed their anticipated Messiah. Starting with the words, "the book of the generation of Jesus Christ…" is an intentional connection back to the Genesis stories that read "these are the generations of…" The basic idea is "the events and people that come from."

When Genesis 6:8 reads "These are the generations of Noah…"), the entire "book" that follows speaks of the people and events from Noah's life and how God intervened. This is the primary way the Hebrew Nation grounded their history. They believed that by looking at past events and people, they were more fully able to understand the present and how God would interact with them.

When Jesus arrived on Earth, went through His life, death, burial, and resurrection, not everyone understood what it all meant. Matthew wants to make it clear that this is the book about Jesus. His life, and all that follows is grounded in how God has intervened in history. None of this is happenstance. God used real people like the ones listed in the genealogies, and real events to make Himself known, culminating with the birth of His Son, Jesus. Those listed were not all great people, not all Jewish people, and some of the events were of the tabloid variety, but God was still present, active, and moving.

What it all means, according to Matthew, is that Jesus is indeed the promised Messiah who has fulfilled the ancient prophecies and has come to bring the Kingdom of God and salvation to the world. What's more is Matthew doesn't hide the warts. In "the book," we see…

The tragedy of Judah and Tamar,

The inclusion of a Canaanite prostitute in Rahab,

The grafting-in of a Moabite woman in Ruth,

The royal lineage continuing despite David's adulterous affair with Uriah's wife, and

The mention of Manasseh, Judah's most vile monarch.

And lest we forget, there is no glossing over what would have been a scandalous birth of the Messiah Himself.

"...and Jacob fathered Joseph the husband of Mary, who gave birth to Jesus who is called the Messiah." Matthew 1:16 (CSB)

The application for us is rich. God interacts in the lives and events of people and the Messianic hope extends to all who will invite Him to intervene in their lives. You may not see it clearly in the moment, but Yahweh is writing a book about you and when it is finished, your story will be one of purpose, grace, mercy, and redemption.

This is the book of _____ (put your name here)

Father, I am truly grateful you are including me in your story. At times I have been ashamed of certain chapters of my life, but I can see how your hand was moving and even in the dark moments, you have never abandoned me. I invite

you to continue to write my story and let each chapter going forward truly glorify you. In Christ's name, amen.

THIRD WEEK OF ADVENT
SATURDAY
"THE BETROTHED"

Reading: Matthew 1:18-25

Now the birth of Jesus Christ was as follows: After His mother
Mary was betrothed to Joseph, before they came together, she
was found with child of the Holy Spirit.

MATTHEW 1:18 (NKJV)

ON SEPTEMBER 24, 1991, I picked up my (then) girlfriend,
Gwen, at her house for what she thought was going to be just
another date night. I had other plans. After dinner, we drove
to the top of a small hill in my 1987 Mazda B2000 pickup
and stopped to view the city lights. Stashed in the bed of the
camper-shelled truck was my guitar and safely nestled in the
center console was an engagement ring I had just paid off and
claimed from layaway at a local jeweler. I grabbed the guitar
and crooned the Willie Nelson song, "Let it be Me," (minus
the nasally twang) to the love of my life. When the song was
complete, I nervously opened the center console hatch, and
with shaky hands picked up the ring case, opened it and asked
Gwen if she would marry me. With a few tears of happiness,
she said "yes," and we rushed off to tell our families that we

were now engaged or, more formally, "betrothed."

Betrothal in Jewish culture was an unbreakable bond, and in the eyes of the community, when the betrothal was announced, the couple was considered married. The Torah was clear that if a betrothed virgin had an affair with another man while engaged, it was a capital crime to be punished and purged from the midst of the community (Deuteronomy 22:23-24).

When Joseph and Mary from Nazareth Village were betrothed, Mary turned up pregnant and Joseph was not the father. Matthew gives us clarity that the pregnancy was a divine act of the Holy Spirit to fulfill the prophecy of Isaiah 7 that a virgin would become the God-bearer and deliver the Christ-child by miracle of the incarnation. This put Joseph in a no-win situation and according to the practice of the day, the ball was in his court as to what would be done with Mary. He could drag his betrothed before the elders for a public trial or do what the Torah permitted and privately give her a bill of divorce. The scandal would remain, but Mary would live. He chose the latter because, as Matthew describes, Joseph was a "just" man – a "righteous" man.

The truth is, one cannot be just and righteous before the Lord without exercising compassion.

> "...the righteous shows mercy and gives."
> Psalm 37:21 (NKJV)

Joseph also stayed in a posture of humility before the Lord. We know this because when God spoke through a dream that explained everything, he listened and humbly submitted to God's plan and purpose, marrying his betrothed. He undoubtedly knew that in a small town like Nazareth, the pregnancy and subsequent birth would be scandalous. There would be talk among the community that the newlyweds would have to endure, but all through this story we see a righteous couple, willing to listen to God, trust Him by faith, and do all that He asked. That is what the Father asks of us. Walk upright, stay humble, do His will, and extend mercy and compassion to all. Through this incredible chain of events, the greatest miracle in history came about. God took on human flesh in the person of Jesus, and He was named Immanuel – God with us.

Father, when I find myself in difficult situations where I am puzzled and perplexed about what to do, may I stay in a posture of humility with an ear that seeks to hear your voice and do things your way. Let my actions toward others, even when I am wronged, always reflect the just, righteous, and merciful God that you are. In Christ's name, amen.

FOURTH WEEK OF ADVENT
SUNDAY
"THE BARREN"

Reading: Luke 1:5-24

...But they had no child, because Elizabeth was barren...

LUKE 1:7a (ESV)

BARREN WOMEN OCCUPY a special place in scripture. From the Matriarchs of Genesis – Sarah, Rebekah, and Rachel – to the mothers of Samson and Samuel, and to the Shunamite woman of 2 Kings, those who are childless capture the heart of God. Infertility in ancient times was a source of shame, and among the people of God, it was a viewed as a sign they lived under a curse, void of God's blessing, and that God was somehow displeased with them. It is interesting, however, barrenness is never announced in scripture unless something miraculous is to follow. God is never in the business of exploiting one's shame to bring about more pain and humiliation. It is His desire to bring healing, fulfillment, and fruitfulness, even out of unfruitful and desolate places.

Zechariah and Elizabeth's story is intricately woven by

Luke into the Advent narrative and mirrors the Old Testament story of Abraham and Sarah. Both couples were advanced in years, and plagued by infertility, yet God visits them in their old age and does what is impossible by human standards – brings forth a child. Yahweh is the only one who brings fruitfulness from barrenness.

Barrenness doesn't always mean infertility, however. It can represent an unfulfilled life, one where hopes and dreams have been stifled, emptiness abounds, and it appears God has withheld his favor and blessing. The good news is, God desires to fill the void and emptiness of our lives, but it isn't always with a public display splashed on the banner headlines of the news. Often, God does His most fulfilling work in the silence and solitude of our barrenness. Paul, quoting Isaiah 54 writes:

> Be glad, barren woman, you who never bore a child; shout for joy and cry aloud, you who were never in labor; because more are the children of the desolate woman than of her who has a husband. Galatians 4:27 (NIV)

How is it even possible to rejoice and anticipate blessing in this state? Inner barrenness is like a desolate wilderness, an empty hole of disappointment and pain. The wilderness is lonely and quiet, but if we allow Yahweh to do His work in the silence and solitude of our harsh wilderness, He can bring a greater satisfaction and fulfillment that we could ever find.

Rejoicing is found in the middle of barrenness if we are patient and content to wait there for God to meet us.

Zechariah was forced into nine months of silence. Elizabeth kept herself in seclusion for five months and during those long months of silence and solitude, God was working and filling a hole in their lives to bring about a fruitfulness they never could have dreamed of. Yahweh was truly up to something great. The angel Gabriel told Zechariah his son would be great, and he would bring them joy and delight. Jesus himself confirmed this and declared there was none greater than John the Baptist – Matthew 11:11. Don't be afraid of a barren wilderness that draws us to silence and seclusion because it can become, as Henry Nouwen said, "the furnace of transformation." That is one of the many beauties of Advent – God moving in desolate places and situations to bring about wonder and amazement.

Father, there are moments in my life when everything feels empty and void of life. In those times, may I see them as opportunities where silence and solitude are drawing me to a place of transformation. Allow me to live with the knowledge that you see me, you see my pain, and you are doing a great work in me. In Christ's name, amen.

FOURTH WEEK OF ADVENT
MONDAY
"THE ANNUNCIATION"

Reading: Luke 1:26-38

"I am the Lord's servant," said Mary. "May it be done to me according to your word."

LUKE 1:38 (CSB)

SEVERAL YEARS AGO, I became friends with a Greek Orthodox bishop in my city. He is a Godly man, and former Pentecostal who moved to the Orthodox tradition as part of a personal quest for a deeper relationship with the Holy Spirit. I found great irony in this as my Pentecostal faith is one that claims to live and operate in the fullness of the Spirit. As the conversations with my friend continued, I discovered the Orthodox Church has a robust view of the Holy Spirit that should cause all Christians, especially Pentecostals, to stand up and take notice. The Orthodox see the Holy Spirit as the person of the Trinity most active in the life and mission of the church. They see the Spirit as the Divine Enabler who empowers us to continuously stretch our lives upward toward the heavens with an insatiable desire to know God deeply. The Spirit also emboldens the people of God to live in His fullness and fulfill God's mission on Earth. Pause, and hold that thought.

A later conversation with my friend turned to Mary, the mother of Jesus. I asked him to explain the Orthodox view of Mary and help me understand why Orthodoxy is accused of "Mary worship." He proceeded to tell me Mary is not worshiped but, rather, honored because she is the full representation of what it means to live in right relationship with God. She is, therefore, the model of the Christian life. While we differ on what this idea looks like in practice, what my friend said about Mary makes perfect sense, especially considering the Annunciation.

When the angel Gabriel appeared to Mary and told her she would conceive and bring forth the Son of God, a very natural response followed: "How can this be since I am a virgin?" Virgins don't conceive and bear children! Gabriel assures Mary this will be a work of the Holy Spirit to bring about the purposes of God through her and that with Him, nothing is impossible.

Now, let's pull our previous thought off the table and connect it to some things from earlier in our Advent journey. Mary, by virtue of the Holy Spirit's work, will bear the seed that will crush the head of Satan. Because of her marriage to Joseph and God's directive to him, the Son who arrives will be named Yeshua, meaning "Savior." He will be the scepter-bearer of Judah who reigns over the house of Jacob from the throne of David with an everlasting Kingdom. Mary's assignment is simply to fulfill the purpose of God through the work of the Holy Spirit and her response sets the standard for all who follow the ways of the Lord: "Be it unto me according to thy word." – Luke 1:38 (KJV)

The implications for us are far-reaching. Yahweh has chosen us to carry out His mission, and the message and example of Mary's Advent experience calls us to never see anything as impossible, including this mission. Mary's story challenges us to align our lives in a posture that invites the Holy Spirit to birth God's purposes *in* us, so they can come *through* us to change the world *around* us. One of my mentors, Pastor Jack Hayford, called this "The Mary Miracle." Our response to all of God's plan is simple: "Be it unto me according to thy word." With such a life, maybe we are more Orthodox than we realize.

Father, today I open my life to new things. I invite your Holy Spirit to come and fill me fresh and new today. I invite your purposes to come alive in my life today recognizing that all things are possible through you and the work of your Spirit in me. May the work that is done in me come forth in power to reveal your salvation to the circle of influence you have given to me. In Christ's name, amen.

FOURTH WEEK OF ADVENT
TUESDAY
"THE GREETING"

Reading: Luke 1:39-45

"...when the sound of your greeting reached my ears, the baby
leaped for joy inside me."

LUKE 1:44 (CSB)

NESTLED IN THE JUDEAN HILLS between Jerusalem and
Bethlehem is the beautiful village of Ein Karem. It is truly a
hidden gem in the land of Israel and home to the Church of the
Visitation, the traditional site where pregnant cousins Mary
and Elizabeth met and enjoyed a joyous time of conversation
and reflection. The cousins were worlds apart not only in age,
but also in socio-economic status. Elizabeth was advanced in
years and her husband, Zechariah, was a priest who served
two tours of duty each year in the temple and was financially
provided for under Israel's tithing system. Indications from
history reveal the priestly class of that day fared well under
this system, lacking little. Though not necessarily wealthy,
their needs were taken care of. Mary, on the other hand, was a
teenager from Nazareth of Galilee where peasant farmers and

craftsmen labored diligently to eke out a meager existence.

Despite these differences, Elizabeth and Mary shared a common bond. Both had become key players in the redemptive plan of God. Inside Elizabeth's womb was the forerunner, the one who would become John the Baptist, the voice crying out in the wilderness. In Mary's womb was the Son of God, the anticipated Messiah for whom John would testify and prepare the way. The turning point of history resided in these two miracle moms. It is unlikely that Elizabeth knew of Mary's pregnancy prior to her cousin's arrival. News traveled slowly in the first century and Luke tells us that after the Annunciation, Mary made plans and hurried to the hill country, wasting no time.

Upon arrival, Luke tells us Mary greeted her cousin. A greeting in that culture was a pronouncement of honor and blessing which invited the shalom of God to rest upon the recipient. Though we are not given the exact verbiage, we are told as soon as the greeting reached Elizabeth's ears, it became the catalyst of two life-giving moments. John leaped with joy in the womb and Elizabeth was filled with the Holy Spirit, all from a simple greeting of the one who carried Christ within her.

When we said "yes" to Jesus, we died to ourselves, and He came to live in us. Christ in us is the hope of glory, not only for us, but also for the world. Herein begins the mission of Christ, with Him living in us. We are carriers of Christ, and as such, the abundant life that only comes through Him now resides within us, but it is not meant to stay there. We carry the presence and power of Jesus to everyone we meet everywhere we go. The life we have within is meant to be given to others. When we greet others, there is an opportunity for more than a handshake, hello, fist bump or high five. We have the capacity to breathe out the life of God to others simply by the words we speak.

I don't want my "greetings" to fuel anxiety or breed fear and discouragement in others. I want my greetings to cause something to come alive in people where they can sense the moving of God's Spirit within them, even if they don't fully understand it. Proverbs tells us…

> Words kill, words give life; they're either poison or
> fruit - you choose. Proverbs 18:21 (MSG)

When we choose to greet through the life of Christ within us, we have the power to bring life and hope into any situation. Our words, like Mary's, can truly bring about miraculous transformation.

Father, today I take stock in the words I speak. I recognize your life is in me, and so many people I greet each day are hurting and broken. Perhaps they have had words spoken to them that have beaten them down. Let my words be well seasoned to raise them up and spark life and hope within. In Christ's name, amen.

FOURTH WEEK OF ADVENT
WEDNESDAY
"THE MAGNIFICAT"

Reading: Luke 1:46-55

And Mary said, "My soul magnifies the Lord, and my spirit rejoices in God my Savior, for he has looked on the humble estate of his servant."

LUKE 1:46-48a (ESV)

IT'S 3:45 A.M. AS I WRITE today's reflection. For the better part of 24 hours, I have been meditating on the song of Mary, known as *The Magnificat* (Latin for "magnify). Across all expressions of Christianity, this Advent hymn is one of the most prayed prayers by the people of God. It has been called subversive by some and revolutionary by others, but it speaks to us of the righteousness and justice of God along with the hope and destiny of humanity. German Pastor Dietrich Bonhoeffer, who was executed by the Nazi regime just days before the end of World War II wrote this of *The Magnificat*.

"This song has none of the sweet, nostalgic, or even playful tones of some of our Christmas Carols. It is instead a hard, strong, inexorable song about collapsing thrones and humbled lords of this world, and the power of God and the power-lessness of humankind." (*The Collected Sermons of Dietrich Bonhoeffer*, Fortress, 2012)

The Magnificat stands as a song of Thanksgiving from the heart of one who has experienced the uplifting hand of God from a desperate situation. Mary magnifies the Lord and rejoices because of what God has done in the past, what He is doing now, and what He will do in the future. Mary gives praise to a God of action, not an aloof deity who is unconcerned with the plight of the oppressed and marginalized. God intervenes on behalf of the hurting, broken, and battered from generation to generation.

The song declares that God "looks with favor" upon humble conditions. The verb indicates Yahweh turns His gaze and locks eyes with the lowly. He notices them! But it doesn't stop with God looking. The Creator then acts upon what He sees. Jesus is the only person in history who got to choose His parents and He chose a lowly couple in an oppressed and obscure region to enter their situation. The Highly Exalted one humbles Himself and becomes low. He fixes His gaze upon the human condition and rewrites the script. The strong and proud are scattered. The mighty are toppled from their thrones. The hungry and needy are satisfied with good things. In this sense *The Magnificat* is subversive and revolutionary but, then again, so is God's Kingdom.

The Kingdom arriving through Mary's child will completely reorder the cosmic reality, rewrite the story of humanity, and make all things new. Jesus likened this Kingdom unto a mustard seed, small and imperceptible, but one that grows into a tree that will cover the earth, providing shelter and nourishment for God's creation.

This seed, as we have anticipated throughout this Advent journey, is destined to bring forth fruit. The Holy Spirit planted the seed in a peasant girl who found favor with Yahweh. She recognized it as a work of God, and her soul could only respond by singing out in praise to God her Savior. Whatever your condition might be, know God sees you and fixes His gaze on you. He stands ready to rewrite the story of your life, giving you a new script to live from. For that, our Lord deserves to be magnified. Find your own *Magnificat* this Advent season as the arrival of our Savior draws near.

Father, we are truly grateful that you pay attention to our lives. You know what is going on and nothing that happens takes you by surprise. We lay our lives humbly before you today and ask that you act on our behalf, doing what only you can do. We pray not only for ourselves, but also those in our world who are oppressed and marginalized, that they too would see you acting on their behalf. In Christ's name, amen.

Reading: Luke 1:57-66

"He asked for a writing tablet and wrote: 'His name is John...'"

LUKE 1:63a (CSB)

"THAT'S JUST HOW WE DO THINGS AROUND HERE!" I am sure at one time or another, all of us have heard that statement. Customs and traditions can be strange animals, and in many cases, these have been in place so long, nobody can remember how or why they were started in the first place. One of my favorite musicals is "Fiddler on the Roof," an early 20th-century story of a Jewish milkman with five daughters who desperately tries to preserve his cultural traditions amid intense pressure to change. Nobody in the milkman's village of Anatevka knew why there was a fiddler on the roof, but it was tradition!

Across the world there are some bizarre traditions. You can look these up, as they are all legitimate.

- An international hair freezing contest in Canada
- A feast for local monkeys in Lopburi, Thailand
- A radish carving festival in Oaxaca, Mexico
- Throwing cinnamon on unmarried 25-year-olds in Denmark
- Groundhog Day in the US (Just watch the movie)
- A food fight using overripe tomatoes in Bunol, Spain
- The ever popular presidental turkey pardon the day before Thanksgiving

It was customary in Jewish culture to name a child after his father or grandfather. This wasn't a commandment in the Torah, but it was the tradition of the community, and a real expectation. In the case of Zechariah and Elizabeth's newborn son, the community was already calling him "Zechariah" after his father. But the boy's parents had a mandate from God that would go against the grain and bypass the tradition. They were to name their son, John (Luke 1:13).

The couple continued to go against the grain of local custom by waiting until the eighth day, the day of circumcision for males, to name their child which was normally done at birth. Elizabeth gave an emphatic refusal to the community, declaring their son would indeed be named John. Tradition continued to press – "No, that is your family name! It's just how we do things around here. Let's ask Zechariah. Surely, as a priest, he will go with the tradition." Zechariah, who had been mute for nine months from his unbelief took a wax-covered writing tablet in hand. With all eyes fastened on the aging priest, he wrote these words: "His name is John."

The son of Zechariah and Elizabeth had already been named John, meaning "God's gracious gift." In that moment, when Zechariah chose God's way over the way of tradition, his hearing and speech were restored, and the community knew John was destined for something great. Indeed, he was. The baby cradled in Elizabeth's arms would become the forerunner of Christ, the voice of one crying in the wilderness in fulfillment of Isaiah's prophecy.

Often in life we will be faced with decisions that force us to choose between the pressures of community and tradition, and what God demands of us. Choosing the latter has the capacity to open our lives up for greater things. Be emphatic with those around you just as Zechariah was and don't be afraid to follow Yahweh's leading. Purpose and destiny are always realized through obedience to the will of God.

Father, I know that following your plan and purpose for my life is not always easy. At times, I feel pressured by those around me to just follow what is popular and culturally acceptable. The pressure intensifies when close friends and family don't understand why I am following a path that seems strange and against the norm, but it is your plan. Allow me to know your voice, be confident, and stand firm in what you are asking me to do. In Christ's name, amen.

FOURTH WEEK OF ADVENT
FRIDAY
"THE BENEDICTUS"

Reading: Luke 1:67-80

Blessed is the Lord, the God of Israel, because he has visited
and provided redemption for his people.

LUKE 1:68 (CSB)

THE MOST POWERFUL TELESCOPE in operation today
is the James Webb Telescope. Launched in 2021 as a joint
operation between NASA, the European, and Canadian Space
Agencies, the Webb Telescope has offered breathtaking views
of stars and galaxies never seen. The power of the Webb lies
in its ability to visually take things that are light years away
and bring them near. The song of Zechariah, known as the
Benedictus (Latin for blessing), is a prophetic telescope boldly declaring the salvation of Yahweh, once far off, has drawn
near. The arrival of the Messiah, patiently expected throughout the centuries, is now at humanity's doorstep, ready to enter its domain.

Zechariah begins the *Benedictus* with standard Hebrew
blessing – "Blessed is the Lord, the God of Israel" and then

shows us the divine telescope by declaring that God has *visited*. This divine act of Yahweh's visitation pulls everything from the distant past into the present. The aged priest, now filled with the Holy Spirit and under divine inspiration, knew the time had come and announced that with God's visitation, a "horn of salvation" had been raised up in the house of David, denoting the royal, saving power of the Messiah.

Probing deeper into the *Benedictus*, we see many of the elements we have witnessed throughout our Advent journey coming together. The promises given to Abraham and David, confirmed by the prophets are now fulfilled in a single visit from God in the person of the Messiah. The time had arrived and the season of waiting, and anticipation was over. Those who have waited and recognized the arrival have been rescued and given the privilege of serving Yahweh "without fear in holiness and righteousness in his presence all our days."

The *Benedictus*, however, has a second verse. Zechariah now speaks to his son, John, and confirms he has a key role to play in the arrival of the Messiah – to prepare His ways by declaring salvation. We already know this, but notice this little twist:

"Because of our God's merciful compassion, the dawn from on high will visit us to shine on those who live in darkness."
Luke 1:78-79 (CSB)

In the first verse of The *Benedictus,* God *has* visited and second verse, he *will* visit. Salvation is not a one and done. It is continuous and the light that came to earth in Bethlehem's manger continues to visit those who are walking in the darkness of this world and lingering in its turmoil. The hope that may seem far away in this very moment is now very near – as near as it was at the time Christ was born.

Yahweh's salvation stands high and above all human thought and imagination, and this is not just an image made visible through a Webb-like telescope. It is a tangible reality made real by the Creator of the universe paying us a personal visit. For that, we sing with Zechariah, "Blessed is the Lord, the God of Israel…"

Father, I can clearly see that your salvation has come near. It is real, and it is tangible because you chose to leave heaven and take on human flesh. I praise you for visiting humanity when you came to earth and glorify you in advance for those moments in the future when your presence will become tangible and real. I worship you today for this marvelous gift that has come to us through your Son, Jesus. In Christ's name, amen.

FOURTH WEEK OF ADVENT
SATURDAY
"THE FULLNESS OF TIME"

Reading: Galatians 4:4-5

But when the fullness of the time had come, God sent forth
His Son, born of a woman, born under the law, to redeem
those who were under the law, that we might receive the
adoption as sons.

GALATIANS 4:4-5 (NKJV)

SEVERAL YEARS AGO, I was at a Christmas party, and on
my table was an ice-breaker question: *"What was the best
Christmas gift you ever received?"* I didn't even have to think
twice for my answer, but there is a backstory.

In January 2006, Gwen and I decided to adopt a baby girl
from Ethiopia. We named her from day one, Charity Tezeta-Noel Jennings, and began the long, arduous adoption process. From the moment we started, our hearts were filled with
hope and anticipation for the day when we would get to hold
our daughter for the first time and bring her home. The journey was cumbersome, and over the next several months, we
built an extensive dossier, completed a home study, filed all
the necessary paperwork with state, federal and international
governments, and then... the waiting began.

Time passed slowly with no word from our agency. Days turned into weeks and the weeks turned into months... Crickets... The hope we had in the beginning was now deferred, and there were no signs the adoption was on the horizon — only promises that it would eventually happen. In September, nine months after the process started, we were in Tanzania with a team from our church when an email from our agency came through, letting us know they had a baby girl for us. Even with the fuzzy dial-up internet of our compound, we were able to see pictures of Charity and the anticipation that springs from hope grew in our hearts. But there was still more waiting, more documents, more time. We found this to be true...

Hope deferred makes the heart sick. Proverbs 13:12 (NIV)

The longer we wait for something hoped for, the more prone we become to despair, and I am sure that is how the people of God felt during those long centuries when the hope of their anticipated Messiah was deferred. There may be hope deferred in your own life right now.

The job
The promotion
The raise
The healing

The reconciliation

The resolution

The promise

The ministry opportunity

Maybe the deferred hope in your life right now is not personal, but rather, for the world. You desire justice for the oppressed and marginalized and grow frustrated because of the lack of progress. Hope is deferred. Perhaps you have reached a point of giving up because in the time between the seed of hope and the arrival of hope, everything is dark and silent. This is why we need to remember the "fullness of time."

Everything about the arrival of Christ was a set time in God's plan. For centuries, God was active, ordering events, and arranging circumstances to prepare the world for the arrival of his Son. History was ready for Christ to be born and all events surrounding the birth of the Messiah fit together perfectly with the promises and prophets of old to fulfill God's redemptive purpose. The seed of hope, promised in the garden and planted in the heart of Abraham arrived in Bethlehem and opened the possibility for us to receive adoption as sons and daughters of God.

The final step in our adoption process was a US Embassy appointment in Addis Ababa, Ethiopia and these were not easy to get. Our agency told us they took the entire month of January off, and if the appointment was not granted before Christmas, it was unlikely to happen until February 2007.

Hope deferred makes the heart sick. We waited. Charity waited.

But on December 10, we received a phone call telling us we had, miraculously, received an embassy appointment for December 26, just two weeks away. Despite the challenges of booking international travel during a holiday season with short notice, on Christmas Eve 2006, we walked into an orphanage in Addis Ababa, Ethiopia and received the best Christmas gift ever: Charity Tezeta-Noel Jennings. The fullness of time came, hope arrived, and the wait was over. For Israel and the rest of humanity, the fullness of time came, and hope arrived in a Bethlehem cave. God sent forth his Son, born of a woman to bring us into his family as His adopted children.

Father, I am grateful that you hold times and seasons in your hand. There are moments when I do not understand your timing for the things in my life that are hoped for. In the confusing time between promise and fulfillment, I pray that I would not lose hope, but lean into you to bring peace to my soul as I wait for the fullness of time. In Christ's name, amen.

CHRISTMAS EVE
DECEMBER 24
"THE BIRTH OF JESUS"

Reading: Luke 2:1-20

I AM A SENTIMENTAL SOUL. Christmas is my favorite holiday, and it always has been. I love the lights, the decorations, the parties, the food, the music, and the movies. (Side note: I am more of a classics guy when it comes to the movies, although I will sit down occasionally and endure, I mean, *watch* a Hallmark Christmas movie with my bride. I will always contend the classic, *White Christmas* is really the original Hallmark Christmas movie).

I recognize that the commercialization of the season can get in the way of the reason for the season, but only if we allow it. I have never had difficulty separating the two mainly because of one thing: the story. The story anchors us in the truth that Advent/Christmas is about God taking on human flesh in the person of His Son, Jesus. In my mind, it is the greatest miracle in history, and a demonstration of God's ability to fulfill his promises. Tonight, on Christmas Eve, the holiest night of the year, the anticipated Savior arrives, and we understand that when we make room for Him, God writes us into the story.

Tonight is truly a holy night where the star of our Savior shines the brightest and beckons all to journey to the manger. It is a night of great joy for all the world because the Lord has come. We pray earth would receive her King and that every heart across the globe will prepare Him room. It is a night where the hopes and fears of all the years come together, and the angels declare peace on earth and goodwill toward men. It is a night that opens the door for all, the rich and the poor, kings, and shepherds, the popular and the marginalized to come to the manger. For in this lowly, humble, animal's feeding trough lay God incarnate, the Messiah. Let the faithful come and adore Him as Christ the Lord. Tonight, the story of God intersects the story of humanity and unto us is born a Savior. *That* is the story.

I encourage you tonight, to allow the power of the story to penetrate the depth of your heart. Find a quiet place alone or, perhaps, with family and friends to simply read the story, just the story. Let it stand in the power of what it is and invite the Holy Spirit to breathe into your heart the sacred mystery of what happened in Bethlehem when the fullness of time came. I offer no additional commentary or application. Tonight is about our hearts making room. I only offer the story in the language I first heard it in as a small boy, the poetic King James. Read it slowly and allow its power to bring joy and peace into your heart. Christ is born!

And it came to pass in those days, that there went out a decree from Caesar Augustus, that all the world should be taxed. (And this taxing was first made when Cyrenius was governor of Syria.) And all went to be taxed, every one into his own city. And Joseph also went up from Galilee, out of the city of Nazareth, into Judaea, unto the city of David, which is called Bethlehem; (because he was of the house and lineage of David:) To be taxed with Mary his espoused wife, being great with child. And so it was, that, while they were there, the days were accomplished that she should be delivered. And she brought forth her firstborn son, and wrapped him in swaddling clothes, and laid him in a manger; because there was no room for them in the inn. And there were in the same country shepherds abiding in the field, keeping watch over their flock by night. And, lo, the angel of the Lord came upon them, and the glory of the Lord shone round about them: and they were sore afraid. And the angel said unto them, Fear not: for, behold, I bring you good tidings of great joy, which shall be to all people. For unto you is born this day in the city of David a Saviour, which is Christ the Lord. And this shall be a sign unto you; Ye shall find the babe wrapped in swaddling clothes, lying in a manger. And suddenly there was with the angel a multitude of the heavenly host praising God, and saying, Glory to God in the highest, and on earth peace, good will toward men. And it came to pass, as the angels were gone away from them into heaven, the shepherds said one to another, Let us now go even unto Bethlehem, and see this thing which is come to pass, which the Lord hath made known unto us. And they came with haste, and found Mary, and Joseph, and the babe lying in a manger. And when they had seen it, they made known abroad the saying which was told them concerning this child. And all they that heard it wondered at those things which were told them by the shepherds. But Mary kept all these things and pondered them in her heart. And the shepherds returned, glorifying and praising God for all the things that they had heard and seen, as it was told unto them. Luke 2:1-20 (KJV)

THE FIRST DAY OF CHRISTMAS
DECEMBER 25
"THE SHEPHERDS"

Reading: Luke 2:8-20

"This will be the sign for you: You will find a baby wrapped
tightly in cloth and lying in a manger."

LUKE 2:12 (CSB)

OUR ADVENT JOURNEY IS COMPLETE! Jesus has arrived, but the festivities have only begun. Today marks the
beginning of the *Twelve Days of Christmas*. When we think of
the 12 days, we default to the cheeky carol by the same name,
but historically, these days leading up to Epiphany on January
6 are days of feasting, rejoicing, and great celebration. Also
known as Christmastide, the 12 days of Christmas give us the
opportunity to reflect on what the birth of Christ means to our
lives.

For the past four weeks with Advent, we have waited with
patience and expectancy for the arrival of the Messiah. We
have walked with the patriarchs and prophets as they received
and proclaimed the promises of Yahweh. We have witnessed
the Creator of the universe continuously intervening in his-

tory, ordering events, and arranging circumstances to bring about the fullness of time. Well now, the fullness of time has come, and Christ is born! God has been made flesh to dwell among us and just as the shepherds on the night of the Savior's birth, "...we have seen his glory..." John 1:14 (NIV).

Now that Christ has arrived, what do we do? We could follow the lead of our culture by looking for the after-Christmas sales, taking down the lights and decorations, and returning the Nativity sets to their boxes for another year and just move on with life. Or, we can take our time and allow the depth and wonder of the greatest miracle in history to penetrate our hearts. God shining his glory around a band of nomadic shepherds camped out on a Bethlehem hillside indicates to us that our Lord wants all of humanity to join with the divine in the same way he joined with us by becoming human.

The good tidings of great joy declared by the angels are for all people and there is something in this familiar story of the shepherds that demands our attention. The angels declared, "you will find a baby..." These lowly shepherds, despised as societal outcasts, had a job to do. They had to move from being passive spectators to being active participants. God wanted them to share in His glory by touching the divine, but they had to go after it, pursue it. And they did. They "hurried off," made haste, and found the baby wrapped up tightly, lying in a manger. They beheld the Son of God, participated in the divine and all they could do in response was testify and give praise to Yahweh for the things they had seen and heard.

Now that Christ is born, God is calling us to make haste, come to the manger and see His glory. As we leave the comfort of daily life and seek, we will find the baby. Once we do, we look upon the divine with wonder, realizing we are now active participants in what God is doing on the Earth. We are the ones who search. We are the ones who seek, but make no mistake, God initiates. Yahweh broke into the world of the shepherds with a grand announcement, and He still breaks into the lives of humanity with the same message.

Today in the city of David a Savior was born for you, who is the Messiah, the Lord. Luke 2:11 (CSB)

Go find Him. God became human so we can participate in the divine.

Father, today I rejoice that Christ was born. I am truly grateful you clothed yourself in humanity in order that we can touch the divine and be joined in relationship to you. Show me in this season of Christmas the far-reaching implications of what this all means. Open new windows of revelation that I may truly see your glory and declare the things I have seen and heard. In Christ's name, amen.

THE SECOND DAY OF CHRISTMAS
DECEMBER 26
"THE NAME"

Reading: Luke 2:21

When the eight days were completed for his circumcision,
he was named Jesus—the name given by the angel before
he was conceived.

LUKE 2:21 (CSB)

FOR THE ANCIENT JEWISH PEOPLE, names held far
more significance than they do in our modern day. We choose
names for our children perhaps because of meaning, following the names of family members or even because we like the
sound. For the Hebrew nation, names spoke of the essence of
the person and in many ways, names were prophetic, fore-
shadowing the destiny of the child. Holocaust survivor and
author Elie Wiesel wrote this of names in the Jewish culture.

"In Jewish history, a name has its own history and its own
memory. It connects beings with their origins. To retrace its
path is then to embark on an adventure in which the destiny of
a single word becomes one with that of a community; it is to
undertake a passionate and enriching quest for all those who
may live in your name." See Arthur Kurzweil, *From Genera-*

tion to Generation: How to Trace Your Jewish Genealogy and Personal History (New York: William Morrow and Company, Inc., 1980), p. 7

The name of Jesus was chosen by Yahweh, announced to Mary and Joseph by angels, and declared to the community eight days after his birth. Jesus (Yeshua) means *"Savior"* and as the angelic announcement proclaimed, He was destined to save His people from their sins. As Wiesel said, the name becomes one with the community and for the followers of Christ, we have the opportunity as a community to live and walk in the power of that name. When the church was launched, Peter boldly affirmed to the rulers, elders, and scribes in Jerusalem:

> There is salvation in no one else, for there is no other name under heaven given to people by which we must be saved.
> Acts 4:12 (CSB)

Paul declared that the name of Jesus is above every name, and at His name, knees will bow, and tongues will confess He is Lord (See Phil. 2:7-11). Demons are subject to His name, and Jesus Himself promised that if we ask anything in His name, He will do it. We baptize others in His name, and the name itself breathes life. In the Revelation, Jesus identifies Himself as the Alpha and Omega, the beginning and the end, the first and the last (Rev. 22:13). This is not by accident. Alpha and Omega are the first and last letters of the Greek alphabet, and with an alphabet, letters are put together to form words, and words convey depth of meaning. We can clearly see throughout God's word that from A to Z, Jesus Christ is God's alphabet, the all-in-all.

A - Author and Perfecter of our Faith (Heb. 12:2)

B – Bread of Life (John 6:35)

C – Chief Cornerstone (Ps 118:22)

D – Deliverer (1 Thess. 1:10)

E – Everlasting Father (Isaiah 9:6)

F – Faithful and True (Rev. 19:11)

G – Good Shepherd (John 10:11)

H – Holy Servant (Acts 4:29-30)

I – Immanuel, God With Us (Isaiah 7:14)

J – Judge of the Living and the Dead (Acts 10:42)

K – King of kings (Rev. 7:14)

L – Light of the World (John 8:12)

M – Mighty God (Isaiah 9:6)

N – Never Ending (Ps. 90:1)

O – Our Living Hope (1 Tim. 1:1)

P – Prince of Peace (Isaiah 9:6)

Q – Quickener of our Lives (Ephesians 2:1)

R – Rock on Which We Stand (1 Cor. 10:4)

S – Savior (Luke 2:11)

T – True Vine (John 15:11)

U – Unchanging (Heb. 13:8)

V – Victorious One (Rev. 3:21)

W – Wonderful Counselor (Isaiah 9:6)

X – eXalted High and Above (Phi. 2:8)

Y – Yahweh – the Lord is One (John 1:1)

Z – Zeal of the Lord (Ps. 69:9)

Jesus is truly our all-in-all, and the Alpha and Omega reminds us that from age to age, He has everything in His hands and by Him, all things hold together. This is the kind of Savior we can fully put our confidence in. Whatever we face, He's got it and there is truly power in the name of Jesus.

Father, you are everything to me. I believe in you but help my unbelief. In my moments of discouragement and doubt, remind me of the indescribable, matchless, undeniable, and priceless name of Jesus. When words fail, I have nothing else to say, I will speak the name of Jesus over every circumstance and situation of my life. Bring a fresh revelation of the name into my soul today. In Christ's name, amen.

THE THIRD DAY OF CHRISTMAS
DECEMBER 27
"THE NEXT RIGHT THING"

Reading: Luke 2:22-24

...They brought him up to Jerusalem to present him to the Lord
(just as it is written in the law of the Lord).

LUKE 2:22-23a (CSB)

THROUGH THE YEARS, I have watched numerous Disney movies with my children and now, my grandchildren. *The Lion King* is my favorite, but there are many others that I have enjoyed including the two installments of *Frozen*. In the second installment of the series one of the main characters, Anna, finds herself reeling from the apparent death of her sister and best friend, Elsa. Battling a wide range of emotions, Anna seeks a way through this dark time in her life and musters the strength to sing a song called *The Next Right Thing*. In Anna's world, that is the only way to overcome her depression and move forward – doing the next right thing, one step at a time.

The idea of doing the next right thing has been attributed to Swiss psychiatrist Carl Jung, poet Elisabeth Eliot, and former US President Theodore Roosevelt. In truth, doing the next right thing originated with God himself.

Do what is right and good in the Lord's sight, so that you may prosper, and so that you may enter and possess the good land that the Lord your God swore to give to your fathers.
Deuteronomy 6:18 (CSB)

Doing the next right thing is to follow God's ways and instructions. Period. If we do this, ultimately, we will come out ahead and enjoy the good things God has for us.

Mary and Joseph, as we have seen throughout this journey of Advent and Christmas, always did the next right thing, following God's plan down to the smallest detail. Now, 40 days after Jesus was born, they took the child from Bethlehem up to Jerusalem to present their newborn son to the Lord, fulfilling what God's law required of them. The next right thing for these brand-new parents involved two things – purification and dedication and through this act of obedience, the Christ child is revealed as the blessing for the entire world.

There is something tucked away in this short moment we cannot ignore. All firstborn males belonged to the Lord, whether animal or human, and had to be consecrated to Yahweh (see Exodus 13:2, 12). Firstborn sons were required to serve the Lord faithfully and ultimately the priests of Israel were given the responsibility to fulfill this role of serving the people on behalf of all firstborn sons (See Numbers 3 and 8).

In the Old Testament, a woman named Hannah brought

her firstborn son, Samuel, and presented him to the Lord (1 Samuel 1:22-28). Samuel stayed in the Tabernacle and became not only a priest, but also a prophet for Israel. Jesus did not stay in the Temple when He was presented yet He became the great High Priest and prophet for Israel, and for the entire world – all because Mary and Joseph did the next right thing.

The Savior of the world declared, "I am the way," and following His way is always the next right thing. Doing the next right thing requires of us a willingness to do things His way, abandoning what we see as right in our natural thinking. In the time of the Judges, everyone did what was right in their own eyes and the results were disastrous. We are seeing this same pattern play out in our modern world as culture sees the next right thing as subjective and dependent on the whim of the individual. When seeking the right thing, we must ask "what is right in the sight of the Lord?" Considering the way of Christ, what is the next right thing?

Mary and Joseph did what was right, and as we will see over the next two days, their next right thing had far-reaching implications. Doing what is right will have ripple effects in our own lives, positioning us for the good things God has for us.

Father, today I pause and repent for seeking next steps within myself. I recognize that your way is better, and I ask you to always keep me close to your word and in a posture that invites clarity regarding every step I take. Next steps that seem right to me can end up disastrous if they are not your steps. May I always do what is right in your eyes. In Christ's name, amen.

THE FOURTH DAY OF CHRISTMAS
DECEMBER 28
"THE NUNC DIMITTUS"

Reading: Luke 2:25-35

Now there was a man in Jerusalem called Simeon, who was righteous and devout. He was waiting for the consolation of Israel, and the Holy Spirit was on him.

LUKE 2:25 (NIV)

PATIENCE IS NOT ONE OF MY GREATEST VIRTUES. Waiting has always created a certain amount of anxiety in my life but, thankfully, the Holy Spirit has not given up on me. He keeps putting me in positions where I am forced to wait and allow the fruit of patience to grow. Sometimes it's at the grocery store where I pick the line with the malfunctioning scanner or in traffic when I choose the wrong lane while navigating rush hour. Other times, I fail to mobile order my coffee and hit Starbucks at the wrong time, encountering a line out the door. Regardless, I must give the Holy Spirit credit for continuing to grow me in this area.

Simeon was an old man carrying a promise that he would not die until he had seen the consolation of Israel, the Lord's Messiah. He patiently waited and eagerly anticipated the moment when he would lock eyes with the Savior of the world. It was Simeon's relationship with the Holy Spirit that allowed this patient expectancy to grow, after all, it was the same Spirit who gave the promise and was upon his life throughout this season of waiting.

On the day Mary and Joseph were doing their next right thing and presenting their firstborn son to the Lord, the Holy Spirit moved Simeon to action. He entered the temple and the moment the aged man looked upon Jesus, he knew his waiting was over, and the promise was fulfilled. Simeon, however, did not rush past this moment and move quickly past the wonder of the Advent. Luke tells us...

> Simeon took him up in his arms, praised God and said..."
> Luke 2:28 (CSB)

"Took him up" does not mean he snatched the newborn infant away from his parents as if to say, "I'll take that. It's my promise!" No. Luke uses a word that means "received." Though every detail is not given, I can imagine an exchange where Simeon declares the promise to Mary and Joseph and politely asks, "May I hold your child?" Mary, supporting the neck of the Son of God gently transfers Him into the waiting arms of a patient man. Pause and reflect on this: Simeon's response to the arrival was to receive the Messiah, Jesus, into his arms and welcome His presence with a song of praise.

Simeon's song, the third hymn recorded by Luke in the

birth narrative, is called the *Nunc Dimittus* (Latin for "now you dismiss") and this short, beautiful song reveals the heart of a man whose soul is at peace with no fear of death because his eyes had seen the salvation of the Lord. With echoes of the Servant Songs of Isaiah, Simeon makes the bold declaration that because of what Yahweh had done in bringing forth Christ as the light to all people, he could depart this life in perfect peace.

For many, the fear of death is real and the uncertainty of what lay beyond this life can foster anxiety in the heart, but it doesn't have to be this way. The Messiah has come and our season of waiting for the one who will conquer death is over. God has brought you to this moment and He is simply waiting for you to open your arms and receive your King. Look into the eyes of Jesus, see the salvation of the Lord, receive it, and allow it to dispel the fear of death. This child is the one who conquers death for all, allowing us to join with Simeon in the *Nunc Dimittus*, knowing we will exit this life with peace.

Father, when I am impatient, remind me that your promises are sure. When I am anxious about this life, remind me that salvation has come. When I am fearful of death, remind me that the one who conquered death is the same promised child who brought salvation to the world. In Christ's name, amen.

THE FIFTH DAY OF CHRISTMAS
DECEMBER 29
"THE PROPHETESS"

Reading: Luke 2:36-38

...She did not leave the temple, serving God ngiht and day with
fasting and prayers.

LUKE 2:37 (CSB)

AGE IS A NUMBER. Ever since I crossed the 50 threshold
a few years back, this has been my 'go to' phrase and it's not
just the coping mechanism of a middle-aged guy. I believe it is
true! I don't feel much different than I did when I was 30, except the recovery time after physical exertion is a little longer.
Thank God for Ibuprofen, aka "Old Man Tic Tacs."

On the day of Jesus's presentation in the temple, there
was a lot of activity and the two people who gave testimony of Christ and his Messiah-ship were well-advanced in
years. Yesterday we met Simeon, and today we meet Anna,
the prophetess. By Luke's account, Anna was over 100 years
old and our brief encounter with this woman of God confirms
my contention that age is only a number. In first century Jewish culture, age was an important factor in being established

as a credible witness. Elders in ancient times were revered. Their testimony mattered because of their long-time devotion to Yahweh, their life experience, and ability to hear the voice of God that only comes through this devotion and experience. Our culture leans in the opposite direction. We tend to view our elders as out of touch relics from a bygone era and seldom regard their testimonies as valid.

Anna was a woman who had fully committed her life to serving in the temple, fasting and prayer. She had undoubtedly seen and heard much in her years of service. The fact that fasting was mentioned indicates a perspective that all was not well, and divine intervention was needed. The temple system had grown corrupt, and the priesthood had deep political and financial ties with Rome which had turned the house of God into a den of robbers who no longer cared for the well-being of Israel, but only for themselves.

Amid this dysfunction was a praying widow who, like Simeon, was in tune with the Holy Spirit, leaning into and listening to His voice. The moment Simeon received the child into his arms and bore his witness, the prophetess gave a second credible witness to what was taking place. She spoke to all who awaited that redemption had indeed come in the person of the Christ child.

Much like the broader culture, a lack among modern-day Christ followers is a respect for the testimony of our elders. The generations before us paid a deep price in serving God's house through prayer and fasting, and we are honored to stand on the shoulders of these giants. The church I serve at has a group of senior adults who, during COVID, started meeting every Wednesday for two to three hours to pray for our church, its ministries, leaders, and our influence in the community. As of the writing of this book, they have only missed four Wednesdays in three years. We owe them deeply and our church would not be the same were it not for their dedication to the house in prayer and fasting. We have dedicated Simeon's and Anna's, men and women of character and commitment who listen to and are led by the Holy Spirit. We need their testimony of Jesus and should never dismiss it because it's experience tested, and it matters. As much as we need the passion of the younger generations, we need the time-honored perspective of Christ that comes from our elders. After all, age is just a number.

Father, we are truly grateful as Christ followers for those who have paved the way for us through a deep commitment to prayer and fasting. Our elders have obtained a credible testimony of Christ because of their devotion and reliance upon your Spirit. May we not only stand on their shoulders, but also follow their example by modeling serving, prayer, and fasting to the next generation. In Christ's name, amen.

THE SIXTH DAY OF CHRISTMAS
DECEMBER 30
"THE LOGOS"

Reading: John 1:1-5

In the beginning was the Word and the Word was with God and the Word was God.

JOHN 1:1 (CSB)

JOHN HAS ALWAYS BEEN my favorite Gospel. I am often asked by those new to scripture where they should start, and I always point them to John. Each of the four gospel writers gives us a unique perspective of the person and work of Christ and John, like a master artist, paints an extraordinary portrait of Jesus as the Son of God. When my students write papers, I ask them to state their thesis up front. I want them to tell me what they want to do in the paper and then prove their point. John does the opposite. He proves his point, and then at the end we get his purpose.

But these are written so that you may believe that Jesus is the Messiah, the Son of God, and that by believing you may have life in his name. John 20:31 (CSB)

John wants us to trust wholly in the fact that Jesus stands alone as the Messiah, and we can only find eternal life through Him. John's claim is bold, subversive, and exclusive, toppling the prevailing Greek and Jewish worldviews of his day. Right out of the gate, Jesus is presented as the *"Word"* (*Logos* in the Greek language). The Word was not only with God in the beginning, He also *is* God. For the Greeks, *Logos* was the wisdom and expression of human reason where true life could be found. John flips this idea upside down and says, "no, Logos is a person" – a person who was active in creating all things and now holds all things together; a person in whom is life and the life in Him becomes the light for all humanity to walk out of darkness.

For the Jews, they would have seen *Logos* as Torah with "in the beginning" as a clear reference to the Genesis creation account. John proclaims the ultimate fulfillment of the Torah is not in the written word, but in a person – Jesus Christ. John magnifies this throughout his Gospel by giving seven statements from Christ Himself that are also subversive and exclusive.

- I am the bread of life (6:35, 48, 51)
- I am the light of the world (8:12)
- I am the door of the sheep (10:7-9)
- I am the good shepherd (10:11, 14)
- I am the resurrection and the life (11:25)
- I am the way and the truth and the life (14:6)
- I am the true vine (15:1-5)

The same "I am" who spoke the world into existence, promising a nation to Abraham and a scepter to Judah; the same "I am" who appeared to Moses in a burning bush and brought a nation out of exile; the same "I am" who gave a kingdom to the house of David and a Savior for all people was born as a human. He is the Word, the Logos, and the only way to find eternal life.

Our world doesn't like this type of subversion and exclusivity. Humanity wants to believe there are universal guiding principles that hold it all together and if we are enlightened enough, we will look inward and find them in our true selves. John declares otherwise and this is what makes the implications of Christ's Advent loom large. Believing Jesus was born is one thing. Understanding what really took place in Bethlehem is another.

Jesus came as God himself to be the way of salvation by shining as a light into a dark world that would not fully understand what is happening. But make no mistake – we do not look to a set of universal principles. We look to a person and by leaning the entire weight of our life on Him, the word, the logos, we find and experience the eternal life of God.

Father, today I pray that you would turn everything in my life upside down that does not recognize you as the way of salvation. Open my eyes to the wonder of what your Son, Jesus, came to do. Forgive me for the times when I have been drawn into the views of the present age that don't see you as the only way and grant me the grace to lean the weight of life on the person of your Son. In Christ's name, amen.

THE SEVENTH DAY OF CHRISTMAS
DECEMBER 31
"THE RIGHT"

Reading: John 1:6-13

But to all who did receive him, he gave them the right to be children of God, to those who believe in his name.

JOHN 1:12 (CSB)

MY CHILDREN HAVE RIGHTS IN MY HOUSE, and they have never had to fight for them. They fought about other things over the years (many, many things), but the rights that come from simply being my kids are theirs. Even as adults, they unapologetically exercise their rights whenever they come over for a visit. They don't need my permission to raid the refrigerator or extract snacks from the pantry. They don't have to ask to use the bathroom or put their feet up on the ottomans. The rights of the house are theirs simply because they were born or adopted into the family.

Our culture fights for its rights. Rights on the broader cultural scale are seen as entitlements because a person, system, or theory granted the rights. When Thomas Jefferson penned the words to the American Declaration of Independence, he wrote of certain inalienable rights that are endowed by the Creator to humanity. Most feel these rights must be protected at all costs, or they will be taken away. Certainly, human rights are worthy of protecting, and we should never arbitrarily abandon them. The good news is, fighting for rights is not the way of Christ when it comes to our new birth and adoption as sons and daughters of God.

Let's put it in the context of the Christmas season we now celebrate. Christ was born in Bethlehem as the light of God to a people groping in darkness. The very name of Jesus, Savior, reveals Yahweh's intention to not only save humanity from sin but also to bring a redemptive way of life to a broken world. We are carriers of Christ's salvation and destined to extend the good news of this redemptive way by becoming faithful witnesses (Simeon's and Anna's) of who Jesus is. This salvation we have been given is found in no other name and once we receive Him as our Savior by calling on the power of His name, He extends to us the right to be and live as children of God. This right is not an entitlement, it is a gift given by virtue of being born and adopted into the family of Yahweh. It is a right we did nothing to deserve and did nothing to earn. We did not fight for the right – Christ did.

The word "right" carries the ideas of permission and authority. Once we received Christ and gave Him access to the "house" of our life and world, He gave us permission to live and exist in his world. It is a privilege, but we do not walk on eggshells in the Father's house. We are children of the Most

High with the right to live as his sons and daughters. This is not a right we take as though it were our own possession. We understand it is graciously and freely given to us by another who ultimately died to give us this right. With that, I demand nothing when I come to Him, but I make myself at home in His house. I feast at His table and enjoy the peace and comfort that can only come from being at home with the Father.

Father, I am humbled by the fact that you graciously adopted me into your family. I have been born again because you sent your Son, and extended salvation to me through his powerful name and, ultimately, his finished work on the cross. I am grateful for the right to live as one of your children and may I honor the family name by honoring you through all my days. In Christ's name, amen.

THE EIGHTH DAY OF CHRISTMAS
JANUARY 1
"THE INCARNATED LIFE"

Reading: John 1:14-18

The Word became flesh and dwelt among us. We observed his glory, the glory as the one and only Son from the Father, full of grace and truth.

JOHN 1:14 (CSB)

I LOVE MEXICAN FOOD, and the spicier, the better. Several years ago, I was home alone and had a craving for chips and salsa. Normally, I make my own salsa but, on this day, I didn't have the ingredients, so I went to the pantry and found a jar of picante sauce. Desperate times call for desperate measures. I grabbed the jar which proceeded to slip out of my hand, shattering on the kitchen floor. Salsa was everywhere – on the cabinets, walls, appliances, etc. It was a mess beyond description. Immediately, I knew what the next hour of my life was going to look like, but in the moment, all I could do was stare at the mess before me, not knowing where to begin.

If you have ever stood over that kind of mess, you understand this reality – you must start somewhere and just dive right into it or it will never get cleaned up. In a sense, this is what happened with the incarnation. The world was a mess of monumental proportions. Humanity's rebellion against God brought sin into the world and wreaked havoc for millennia. None of humankind's self-driven efforts made a dent in the mess. But God did not stay in heaven, scratching His head, looking at the mess saying, "someone should do something about that." No, the Creator of the universe clothed Himself with human flesh in the person of Jesus and came right into the middle of the mess to do something about it.

This is the true miracle of Christmas, and it was done to raise humanity out of its own depravity, to a position of being seated with Christ in heavenly places (See Ephesians 2:1-6). In the 11th century, Anselm of Canterbury reflected on this.

"In the incarnation of God, there is no lowering of Deity; but the nature of man we believe to be exalted."
(Anselm - *Cur Deus Homo*)

To raise us up, Christ demonstrated the true nature of His Kingdom by taking on the nature of a servant. In the fourth century, Athanasius of Alexandria put it this way:

"The Lord did not come to make a display. He came to heal and teach suffering men. For one who wanted to make a display the thing would have been just to appear and dazzle the beholders. But for him who came to heal and to teach the way was not merely to dwell here, but to put himself at the disposal of those who needed him." (Athanasius – *On the Incarnation*)

The implications for us are enormous. As followers of Jesus, the incarnation challenges us to live an incarnated life – the kind of life that refuses to just stand back and look at the mess of the world but jump into the mess and put ourselves at the disposal of those who need us. We must be willing to enter the brokenness and dysfunction of those we serve, bringing the healing that came through Christ. It is not enough to have the core doctrines of faith committed to memory. The true mark of our discipleship is action that flows with love from Godly character. We have received grace upon grace from his fullness, and now we become dispensers of that grace by living an incarnated life. Christmas joy, thus, becomes a Christmas challenge.

The word became flesh and blood and moved into the neighborhood. We saw the glory with our own eyes, the one-of-a-kind glory, like Father, like Son, Generous inside and out, true from start to finish.
John 1:14 (MSG)

Father, as we reflect on the wonder of the incarnation, may we as your people resolve to live an incarnated life. Forgive us for being self-absorbed, shaking our heads at our broken world and expecting someone else to clean up the mess. You did your part by establishing the way and you passed the assignment unto us. Allow us to continuously put our own lives at the disposal of others. In Christ's name, amen.

THE NINTH DAY OF CHRISTMAS
JANUARY 2
"THE OUTSIDERS"

Reading: Matthew 2:1-12

...And there it was—the star they had seen at its rising.
It led them until it came and stopped above the place where
the child was.

MATTHEW 2:9 (CSB)

THERE IS PROBABLY NO SEGMENT of the Christmas story that has been more influenced by tradition than the visitation of the Magi. Christmas cards, artwork and, of course, the song suggest three Magi visiting the Christ child, but the scripture never says there were three. Early Christian traditions place the number as high as 12. Try fitting that into your nativity set!

One of my favorite newspaper cartoons growing up was *The Far Side* and I recall seeing one of those cartoons depict a Magi leaving the place where Jesus resided with Mary closing the door behind him. The caption read, "Unknown to most Biblical Scholars, there was a fourth wise man who was turned away for bringing a fruit cake." The truth is, it's highly unlikely that the Magi made it to the cave the night Jesus was born which is why the feast of Epiphany is traditionally celebrated two weeks after Christmas Eve.

It is possible that the Magi were Zoroastrian Priests from the region of Persia who were steeped in the magic arts, astronomy, and astrology. They believed the stars predicted the future and foretold one's fate, but there was something unique about the star of Bethlehem. In ancient times, those who studied the stars believed that a special, bright, and luminous star appeared every time someone of significance was born. Perhaps as scholars, the Magi were versed in other cultures, and it is possible they were familiar with this ancient Jewish prophecy regarding their Messiah.

> I see him, but not now; I behold him, but not near. A star will come out of Jacob; a scepter will rise out of Israel....
> Numbers 24:17 (NIV)

As they surveyed the bright night of the Persian sky and saw the star, something inside of the Magi knew this one was special and that a king had been born. They assembled their travel party and headed west, journeying 1,000 miles on roads you and I would never travel on, patiently riding over mountains and deserts, crossing rivers and valleys until they arrived in Jerusalem inquiring of the one born King of the Jews. Now, why would Matthew, a Jew, include a story in his narrative written primarily to a Jewish audience about a group of outsiders?

Matthew wants his Jewish audience to know they aren't the only ones who will benefit from the life of their Messiah. Here, Matthew portrays Jesus, even as an infant, shattering religious tradition by bringing outsiders in to share in the joy of his Advent. Throughout his life, Jesus shattered other traditions regarding race, gender, and class touching other outsiders as well. The poor and marginalized, lepers, prostitutes, and even Roman centurions were invited to join Christ at His table. The coming of the Magi is part of the wonderful reminder that everyone is welcome in the presence of the King.

You may feel at this moment as though you are on the outside looking in when it comes to God. Because of your station in life or personal history, you wonder if Yahweh will love and accept you or hold you at a distance. Keep following the star because it is drawing you to God's loving kindness. We are told in the narrative that the star "led them until it came and stopped above the place where the child was." In a supernatural act, God moved the star ahead of the Magi, proving God will do everything He can to help us find Him. The Magi knew this was no ordinary star and no ordinary King. At the same time God was drawing them, the Magi were looking and when it all converged, these outsiders came face to face with the Holy One of Israel, the Savior of all the world.

Father, I am grateful that you have drawn me with your grace and loving kindness. I pray today for those who are still seeking. May they see your star moving in their lives to lead them to you and your salvation. I pray the fear and inadequacies that keep people at a distance would be dispelled from their lives, and that they will come face to face with their Savior, embracing his love, and reveling in his grace. In Christ's name, amen.

THE TENTH DAY OF CHRISTMAS
JANUARY 3
"THE GIFTS"

Reading: Matthew 2:11

They entered the house and saw the child with his mother,
Mary, and they bowed down and worshiped him. Then they
opened their treasure chests and gave him gifts of gold,
frankincense, and myrrh.

MATTHEW 2:11 (NLT)

ONE OF THE CHRISTMAS HIGHLIGHTS for us has always been watching the kids and now, grandkids, open their gifts. Seeing their faces light up when they receive a gift they were hoping for is such a delight, reinforcing the truth that it is far better to give than to receive. A few years ago, Gwen and I started our own 12 days of Christmas tradition where we buy each other 12 gifts leading up to Christmas Eve. Granted it's backwards from the church calendar, but it's okay! We have loads of fun. Most of the gifts are small but meaningful, and there is the one "big" gift on Christmas Eve. The first year we did it, each morning I hid the gift somewhere in the house and wrote riddles on cards that Gwen had to solve to find the gift. It was an incredible experience filled with laughter that brought us closer together in our marriage, all through the giving of gifts.

When the Magi completed their journey, they first worshiped the newborn King and then, reached for their treasure chests. As homage and worship were offered to the Christ child, they gave gifts from their treasure of gold, frankincense, and myrrh. Speculations abound regarding the symbolic meaning of the gifts, but the key is, they gave. Some translations of this story use the word "offered" instead of "gave" and the word is used elsewhere in scrpture to describe a sacrificial gift or offering. The Magi gave sacrificially out of the abundance of their treasure to the King. As we near the end of our Advent/Christmas journey and ponder how we should live in the wonder of the incarnation, I would like to offer a simple question for all of us to consider:

"What's in your treasure chest?"

Imagine the scene on Christmas morning if you just wrapped up empty boxes of all sizes and shapes, decorated them with elegant wrapping, neatly tied them with a red Christmas bow, and placed them under the tree. Then imagine the look on a child's or loved one's face when they open the boxes and nothing is there. Next, imagine the Magi opening empty treasures before the King. Now…think of your own life.

What's in your treasure chest? What is in the storehouse of your life that is worthy of giving to the King? Jesus told the religious leaders of his day what was in their treasure chest.

> ...You are like whitewashed tombs, which look beautiful on
> the outside but on the inside are full of the bones of the
> dead and everything unclean.
> Matthew 23:27 (NIV)

The more we mature in Christ, the more we will understand that what's on the inside trumps what is on the outside. As we continue to grow in our faith, the things that are dead and unclean in our hearts will give way to things alive and pure, making the treasury of our life full, complete, and ready to give away. Our Lord put it this way:

> Every student of the Scriptures who becomes a disciple in
> the kingdom of heaven is like someone who brings out new
> and old treasures from the storeroom.
> Matthew 13:52 (CEV)

As we walk in discipleship, we will offer God old treasures from the deep depository of our lives that have built up in Him through the years, but we will also stay in a posture that invites the new and fresh to come. We never throw out the old, but we welcome the new and when we come to the Lord to worship, we open this wondrous treasure within and present it to Him for his good use. God will always use what we have, but we never want to go before Him with an empty treasure chest. Your life is a gift, and there is no greater example of following Christ than to model your life after a God who so loved the world, that he gave this only Son (John 3:16). I ask again: what's in your treasure chest?

Father, I long to give you my best in all things. I never want to fall into the trap of allowing my life to look great on the outside but having no treasure on the inside. As I walk with you, I open my life to all that being a disciple means – being with you, becoming like you, and ultimately doing what you did. Continue to build the storehouse of my life and continue to do new things within my life each day. In Christ's name, amen.

THE ELEVENTH DAY OF CHRISTMAS
JANUARY 4
"THE DARK SIDE OF CHRISTMAS"

Reading: Matthew 2:16-18

A voice was heard in Ramah, weeping, and great mourning,
Rachel weeping for her children; and she refused to be
consoled, beceause they were no more.

MATTHEW 2:18 (CSB)

JUST OUTSIDE THE WALLS of modern-day Bethlehem, on the road to Jerusalem, is the tomb of Rachel. Tradition holds that when the children of Israel were set to be deported to Babylon, they gathered in Ramah, the site of Rachel's tomb, and began their long journey to exile. Jeremiah the prophet, quoted by Matthew, first spoke of Rachel weeping for her children as the people were forced from their homeland. Matthew sees another perspective and uses Jeremiah's prophecy to convey the emotion surrounding the dark side of the Christmas story. The dark side of Christmas is neither celebrated nor made part of our Christmas pageants. It is the tragic story of a paranoid ruler, imperial control, an evil agenda, senseless murder, grief, sorrow, and lamentation.

When Herod unleashed his soldiers into the tiny village

of Bethlehem and took the lives of innocent infant boys, Rachel once again wept for her children and refused to be consoled. The injustice of this moment cannot be explained away or glossed over as if it never happened. The dark side of Christmas marks a unique dichotomy for the followers of Jesus, for it invites us to share in Rachel's pain while concurrently recognizing that hope has arrived. Creation may be groaning under the thumb of evil and injustice but, at the same time, a new world has come, and redemption is on its way.

This is exactly what it means to live in the now and not yet of God's Kingdom. The Kingdom has come, and we live in the "now" under the rule of the King who was born. But contrary to the words of the song, the night is not silent. All is not calm, and all is not bright. There is abundance of pain and suffering across our world as we live in the "not yet," anticipating the King's second Advent when the fullness of the Kingdom will be revealed, and all will be made right.

It is striking that Luke gives us the *Benedictus*, the *Magnificat*, and the *Nunc Dimittus* while Matthew gives us the song of Rachel's pain. Here's why. When God does something new in the Earth, there is always pushback, and this conflict will continue until the day Christ returns and every tear will be wiped away. The message we carry in the interim is this: When tragedy strikes and bad things happen to good people; when injustice continues to oppress and rule the day, we join with those in anguish. We weep with Rachel who has suffered loss, all the while clinging to the hope of Advent that a new day has indeed come, and a new day will come.

> He will wipe every tear from their eyes, and there will be
> no more death or sorrow or crying or pain. All these things
> are gone forever.
> Revelation 21:4 (NLT)

Most scholars contend the population of Bethlehem at the time of Christ was probably around 1,000. Given this size, it is probable that about 20 male infants under the age of two were murdered by Herod. These are revered in some expressions of Christianity as the first martyrs who will rise with us at the last day, triumphant and whole because the King for whom their lives were lost, conquered death for all. As we walk the line in our day between despair and hope, we never let go of hope, but holding the hand of Rachel, we sit and weep with her, lamenting the losses that come through the evil and injustices of our day. We are in this together.

Father tune my ears into the cries of those who lament. Open my eyes to those who suffer loss. Let my feet walk with compassion beside those who grieve and mourn. May my actions be loud, and my words be few as I sit in the pain with those who are hurting. At the same time, let the hope you bring emanate from my life and become a balm of healing for all. In Christ's name, amen.

THE TWELFTH DAY OF CHRISTMAS
JANUARY 5
"THE RETURN"

Reading: Matthew 2:13-15; 19-23

...Get up, take the child and his mother, and go to the land of Israel, because those who intended to kill the child are dead.

MATTHEW 2:20 (CSB)

I WILL NEVER FORGET my first panic attack. The circumstances surrounding the attack require more space than a devotional allows, but it all centered around having to return to a place where something traumatic had happened in my life. Memories are powerful and they have the capacity to trigger a full array of emotions on the inside, especially when we are forced to face our past.

When the angel appeared to Joseph in a dream expressing the urgency to leave Bethlehem for Egypt, it was enough to strike fear into the heart of any parent. Herod's brutality was well-known to all in the region and, certainly, Joseph understood the gravity of the situation. When the angel said "Herod is about to search for the child to kill him…" it conveyed that the tyrant's plot was imminent, and Joseph had no time to waste. Fear, perhaps nauseousness, and a stressful pit in the stomach must have come upon the young parents as they packed their belongings, the gifts from the Magi and made haste to Egypt. It probably wasn't until after they arrived that the anxiety of the situation left, and they were able to resume some sense of normalcy. Traumatic experiences, however, take time to recover from.

We are not told how long the family stayed in Egypt but at some point, after Herod's death, Yahweh deemed it safe for them to return. The return could not have been easy, even with God's blessing. I can envision as the family drew near to the Judean hills surrounding Bethlehem there was a sense of panic, fear, and uncertainty. It would not be a stretch to assume Joseph was triggered by the familiar feelings of helplessness once he heard that Herod's son, who was equally as brutal as his father, now held power. Returning to a traumatic place with the prospect of more trauma was more than Joseph could bear and Matthew tells us, "he was afraid to go there."

Once again, God intervened, spoke to Joseph through a dream and told him to go to Galilee. Going back to the region of Galilee was another apprehensive return for the young couple, for it was the place where Mary's scandalous pregnancy occurred. People have long memories, especially in small towns, but Joseph and Mary were able to return to Nazareth, face their past, and set up a life for themselves and their son. It proved to be a good thing. Luke tells us of Jesus in Nazareth...

The boy grew up and became strong, filled with wisdom, and
God's grace was on him.
Luke 2:40 (CSB)

With God's guidance and help, we can face our past head-on, no matter how traumatic it might be. God will never steer us into harm's way, and we can rest knowing there is a fruitful life under His care waiting for us whether in Egypt or Nazareth. God's plans cannot be stopped, and He will always give us the grace we need in the season we need it. When I had my panic attack on that lonely stretch of Arizona highway, I had to stop, pray, and lean into the Holy Spirit. He gave me the strength to face my past trauma head-on and allowed me to experience a fresh touch of his presence along the way. Don't fear the return. God is with you.

Father, you always see the end from the beginning, and you know all my days past, present and future. Because I am your child, you have my best interest in your very heart, and you do not want me chained to the traumatic events of my past. Give me the grace to face those things in the power of your Spirit with your Holy presence guiding me. I declare that trauma won't win, and your purposes will be fulfilled in my life. In Christ's name, amen.

EPIPHANY
JANUARY 6
"THE REVELATION"

Reading: Isaiah 60:1-6

Arise, shine, for your light has come, and the glory of the LORD shines over you.

ISAIAH 60:1 (CSB)

TODAY MARKS THE END of our Advent/Christmas journey with the celebration of Epiphany. Epiphany means "appearance" or "manifestation" and celebrates God revealing Himself to the world in the person of Jesus. The earliest traditions of Epiphany honor any of these four manifestations of Christ, all of which are worthy of celebrating:

- His Birth
- The Visitation of the Magi
- His Baptism
- His First Miracle at the Wedding in Cana of Galilee

At His birth, the angels testified of the one who appeared as the Savior, fulfilling the promises made to Israel. The visitation of the Magi demonstrated God manifesting His glory to all humanity and drawing them to salvation. At Jesus' baptism, the Spirit descends, and the Father speaks from heaven revealing and confirming Jesus's identity as the Son of God. With the wedding at Cana, Jesus is manifest as the one who has authority over all things. The bottom line: God has appeared to us in the person of Jesus Christ and if we have seen Him, we have seen the Father. If we want to know what God is really like, we look at Jesus, the Son, who has been made manifest as the light of the world. Our light has come, and God's glory has risen upon those who prepared room and received him.

Light not only speaks of the nature and character of God, but it also speaks of the inner serenity and quality of life that comes from living in the light of His glory. On this day of Epiphany, we can arise and shine radiantly because His light has appeared and been made manifest in our hearts. When we chose to receive Jesus as the Lord and leader of our life, we received God's light which emanates from His glory revealed in the Son and is now given to us as our glory – the light of life.

For God, who said, "Let there be light in the darkness," has made this light shine in our hearts so we could know the glory of God that is seen in the face of Jesus Christ.
2 Corinthians 4:6 (NLT)

As we bring this wonderful season to a close, be encouraged that you no longer need to hide in the shadows or stay stuck in the dark, hidden places of your life. The light of God that shines in our hearts through Christ is never to expose our shame, but to bring us to His healing touch. We can live in full view of His light, allowing all the fears of our past to be removed. Whenever we feel darkness trying to once again take over, we boldly say: "No! I will arise and shine because my light has come. His glory is risen on me through Christ, and I invite His light to shine forth in every step I take."

The message of this season is 100% Jesus…Born unto you as a Savior and shining as a star that draws all to Him. The Son of God who holds authority over all things past, present, and future, invites all to come. This is our Epiphany!

Father, we are truly grateful for this season of Advent and Christmas. Today, as we celebrate Epiphany, remind us of the true light that has come into the world through your Son. You have called us out of darkness to live and walk in the light that has come to us. We commit our lives to you anew this day and invite you to shine brightly through us. May our lives always reflect your glory and draw others to your salvation. In Christ's name, amen.

ACKNOWLEDGEMENTS

There are so many people in my life that made contributions to this work. This is by no means an exhaustive list, and the words that follow cannot fully express my gratitude to these incredible individuals, but they come from my heart.

To my wife and family for believing in me. Without them, this book would have never happened.

To my sister, Julie Miser, for her tireless work on the graphics and formatting. She is a true pro.

To my editor, Judy Hilovsky, for helping me understand how to use the word "that."

To everyone who walked with me all the way through my dark night of the soul. You know who you are, and I am grateful for your friendship.

To my dad, Gene, for always modeling the way of Christ.

Finally, to my mom, Patricia, who is watching from heaven. Your passion for scripture was imparted to me when I was a young boy. I miss you....

Made in the USA
Columbia, SC
13 November 2024